Praying
the Movies II

More Daily Meditations from Classic Films

EDWARD N. McNULTY

D1364977

Westminster John Knox Press
LOUISVILLE • LONDON

Scripture quotations, unless otherwise indicated, are from the New Revised Standard Version of the Bible, copyright © 1989 by the Division of Christian Education of the National Council of the Churches of Christ in the U.S.A., and used by permission.

Scripture quotations marked CEV are from the *Contemporary English Version,* Copyright © by the American Bible Society. Used by Permission.

"When Love Is Found," the hymn by Brian Wren, is copyright © by Hope Publishing Co. The excerpt on page 197 from "When Love Is Found" is used by permission of Hope Publishing Co.

Book design by Sharon Adams
Cover design by designpointinc.com

First edition
Published by Westminster John Knox Press
Louisville, Kentucky

This book is printed on acid-free paper that meets the American National Standards Institute Z39.48 standard. ♾

PRINTED IN THE UNITED STATES OF AMERICA

03 04 05 06 07 08 09 10 11 12 — 10 9 8 7 6 5 4 3 2 1

Library of Congress Cataloging-in-Publication Data
McNulty, Edward N., 1936-
   Praying the movies II : more daily meditations from classic films / by Edward N. McNulty.—1st ed.
       p. cm.
   ISBN 0-664-22661-2
   1. Motion pictures in church work. 2. Motion pictures— Religious aspects—Christianity—Meditations. I. Title: Praying the movies 2. II. Title: Praying the movies two. III. Title.

BV652.82.M36 2004
242—dc21   2003049704

Contents

Introduction

"Confessions" in the Dark by a Film Lover

Whenever I lead a session on film and the church, someone almost always asks me how I, a clergyman, became so involved with films. I think sometimes the questioners mean, "How did a good Presbyterian boy, a representative of a Reformed tradition that once banned images from the sanctuary, get mixed up with the product of Hollywood Babylon?" (Actually, at the oral examination for my doctor of ministry degree on art, film, and Christ at Dayton's United Theological Seminary, the faculty theologian Dr. Tyrone Inbody used almost those exact words, though half jokingly.) So, let me indulge in a bit of autobiographical nostalgia. Maybe some of what follows will be relevant to your own journey in the Spirit. If you think not, then go on and skip ahead to the more immediately relevant "Using This Book" section of the Introduction.

My love for the movies predates my love for God by several years. Some of my fondest memories as a boy involve movies. In those pre-television days my father, a great tinkerer with all things electronic, bought a

16-mm sound movie projector and turned our basement into a minitheater several times a month. Usually
his tastes ran to musicals and comedies, especially if the
latter starred Bing Crosby or Bob Hope, but he liked
cowboy films too. Often what were available were the
B-grade films, with stars such as Gene Autry, Roy
Rogers, "Wild Bill" Elliott, or Randolph Scott, these
being relatively cheap to rent. My movie experience
was not confined to the basement, however. On a
Friday night after our family grocery shopping at the
A&P, I looked forward to eating out with my parents.
We would peruse the newspaper movie ads for the
neighborhood theaters while waiting for our orders to
arrive. I always put in my two cents' worth for a war or
action film, but even if the main feature was one of
those "mushy" Ingrid Bergman-Humphrey Bogart
movies, there was always the second feature to enjoy.
The latter was often a Charlie Chan murder mystery
or other such kid-pleasing flick—and the popcorn was
actually affordable then, even for a kid on an
allowance. I loved it when we went to the Zaring
Egyptian Theater because passing through its ornate
doors was like entering an ancient Egyptian temple, its
walls embellished with statues of bizarre beings and
exotic paintings. Even this neighborhood theater fostered the imagination of its patrons, unlike the
unadorned boxes that pass for theaters today.

Movies stirred my imagination and gave me things
to dream about. When I was in kindergarten my prized
possession was my Gene Autry outfit, with its "genuine
leather" holster and shiny six-shooter that fired caps.
During the next few years we boys got into serious
arguments, as passionate at times as medieval monks
arguing about dancing angels and pinheads, over who
was really "King of the Cowboys"—Roy Rogers or

Gene Autry. Roy finally won our allegiance when we heard tales from our parents of Autry's drinking. Also by then we were old enough to appreciate pretty Dale. On hot summer afternoons we loved going to the wading pool with towels tied around our necks to make capes, turning us into the crime-fighting heroes we cheered Saturday afternoons as we thrilled to the ten-part serial adventures at our neighborhood theater.

When my boyhood innocence came to an end with the divorce of my mother and dad, movies provided an enjoyable alternative to harsh reality: couples might separate in the movies, but they always rushed into each others' arms again just before "The End" appeared on the big screen. And on the frontier of the Westerns they stuck together (if there was a woman in the picture) because they had to in order to overcome their hostile environment. During my junior high school years I worked at a downtown newsstand, and thus never lacked the quarter cost of a ticket. In those days there were about eight theaters in downtown Indianapolis, so there was always a movie showing that I wanted to see. Along with books, movies transported me, as Dorothy sang, "Somewhere Over the Rainbow." It was a good place to be. There I was not just a helpless kid unable to bring a mother and father back together again, as in Disney's *The Parent Trap*. (For a while I thought this might happen when my parents came together to visit me in the hospital when I had appendicitis.) Instead I was a fast-drawing cowboy taking the side of the underdog, or a swashbuckler setting to right a people oppressed by an evil governor or king. By then John Wayne had replaced Gene Autry and Roy Rogers for me. There seemed to be no problem he could not solve or bad guy he could not best in a brawl.

In high school I began to see some of the "problem movies" Hollywood produced in the late '40s and '50s. *Gentleman's Agreement* made me aware that my grandmother's favorite term to describe obtaining a bargain ("I sure Jewed him down!") was insultingly wrong. In *Broken Arrow* I was introduced to Indians who were noble and honest, not greedy and savage like the white settlers opposed to them. *Pinky* showed me the anguish of a mixed-race girl harboring a secret that could destroy her happiness. *Cry, the Beloved Country*, the first Sidney Poitier film I saw, deeply impressed me with the need to do something about racial prejudice. My favorite science fiction film at the time, *The Day the Earth Stood Still*, boldly stated that *we*, not evil space aliens, are the main obstacle to world peace. A little before this *The Boy With Green Hair* made me aware that world peace, not military victory over foreign foes, was something we should strive for. I should mention that during these years science fiction itself provided me with great relief from the realities of a broken family—not just the stories themselves, but fellow readers who banded together into clubs and attended sci-fi conventions. I edited and published our club's mimeographed magazine—"fanzines" they were called—and loved receiving stories and artwork from contributors and letters from readers. My first movie review appeared in its pages, a scathing put-down of a preposterous movie about giant ants attacking humanity entitled *Them*.

It was seminary that turned me on to seeing film through theological eyes—though perhaps at this point I should back up and describe when my second love began, that involving God. I was not raised in the church by pious parents. My mother was indifferent to the church, and my father was outright hostile to all things clerical. His family of Irish Catholics had turned against the church when a priest in rural northwest Pennsylvania tried to tell my great-grandfather how much he was going to pay to the church that year. Family legend records that Great-Granddad ordered the priest off the farm with his shotgun. Thus I can recall my father cynically remarking many times how all preachers were interested in was your money. However, when I was around eight years old, neither parent raised objections when I gave in to the repeated invitations of my best friend to accompany him to the little mission church he had started attending. It was headed by a carpenter lay preacher who drove his station wagon around to pick up whomever was willing to attend. I learned a lot about God and Christ at the Grace Brethren Church and sang some rousing old gospel songs and hymns that never came close to making it into the Presbyterian Hymnal. The gospel preached there was a mixture of fear and love. Depictions of hell at times gave me nightmares as I saw my parents being consigned to its fiery depths. But the claims of God's love for all stretched my little boy's conception—I remember how surprised I was to hear the preacher state that God loved our Japanese enemies as well. (My conception was shaped by war movies of John Wayne gleefully shooting and bayoneting them.) But as I grew a bit older and encountered a crisis of faith over my parents' divorce and the troubling questions raised by grade school science, I drifted away from church for a few years.

I will not bore you with the details of my faith crisis, or go into how the theology of the church into which I was baptized (not only by immersion, but in a *river!*) could not satisfy a questioning young mind. Nor of how another friend led me back to the church, a

Methodist one that did not require members to check their minds at the door, but one that encouraged questions instead. At this church, and at college, I was introduced to a God who loved me no matter what and who regarded doubt as an integral part of a growing faith. It was a God who was beckoning me to enter the ministry because the very experiences that had been so painful could be used in reaching others going through a similar experience. At seminary I recall one of our professors urging us to go see the film version of what had been one of his favorite plays, *West Side Story*. We did, and the music, the dancing, and the drama mesmerized us. It was true, as he had pointed out, that the Jets and the Sharks were for their members the equivalent of the church, enabling them to hang onto their sense of self-worth ("walk tall") and providing them with community ("you're never disconnected"). In the hauntingly beautiful "Somewhere There's a Place For Us" we saw not only the yearning of two lovers but a reflection of the longing of Israel and all of broken humanity for "a new way of living, a way of forgiving," fulfillable only in Christ's teachings about the kingdom of God.

The films of Ingmar Bergman and Federico Fellini were just coming out then, too, and were readily available in the Chicago of my McCormick Seminary. Though we often had to struggle to understand them at times, something which only a few American films made us do then, we found them exciting. One of the great teachers at McCormick was Professor John Burkhart, whose course "Man in Modern Literature" especially equipped me to approach film as well as novels. From a theological perspective I learned that God did not have to be named in order to permeate a work of art, that "nothing in all creation" (see Rom. 8:37–39) was beyond the pale of the often-nameless Deity whose greatest symbol of love was a cross. We discovered that this cross could take many and strange forms, such as in Graham Greene's great novel *The End of the Affair*, when the adulteress Sarah gives up her lover in order to follow God; or in *The Power and the Glory*, when the whiskey priest returns to certain arrest and death because he had been told that a dying man wanted to make his confession.

Equipped with a theology informed by Bonhoeffer and such polar opposites as Barth and Tillich, as well as by theologians working in literature, such as Amos Wilder and Nathan Scott, I set forth into the plains of North Dakota to serve the church as a pastor. There was a movie theater in our small town, but except for an occasional *Man for All Seasons* or *Days of Wine and Roses*, it seldom offered challenging fare. Certainly not Bergman or Fellini. I followed in my father's footsteps (though I didn't think of it as this at the time) by renting 16-mm feature films—at least when I could find a group willing to put up the $150 to $200 cost. My little church could not afford this amount, nor would the proceeds of the evening offering match the figure. Thus I found that community groups wanting to explore an important issue were a good source of funding. It was the '60s, and film studies were becoming popular. Films Incorporated sent out an attractive brochure aimed at pastors and educators. They had contracted with a Methodist associate pastor, G. William Jones, to select one hundred of their films for discussion-guide treatment. He called the program "Dialogue With the World," and for each of the films that a church or group rented, one of the discussion guides was sent free. It was enlightened capitalism at its best. I am sure I was but one of a thousand or more pastors who benefited from this wonderful program of film study.

Late in the '60s Jones wrote the book that really convinced me I was on the right road in approaching film as parable—*Sunday Night at the Movies*. It was accompanied by a flurry of books over the next few years: *Celluloid and Symbols, Church and Cinema, Popcorn and Parable, Film Odyssey*, and a host of film books from Pflaum Press, including works by Pierre Babin and William Kuhn. Robert Short's exciting books probing the theology underlying Charles Schulz's *Peanuts* came out then, again providing us with clues for decoding the arts theologically. Corita Kent, then known as "Sister Corita," was creating her theological serigraphs and writing about the arts, as were Harvey Cox and Malcolm Boyd. Dennis Benson in his books and workshops showed us that even pop and rock music contained gospel insights. He led many of us into producing our own multimedia presentations, and my collection of kit rentals called "Visual Parables" was born and eventually used by several hundred churches in their contemporary worship services and youth retreats.

It was Dennis who encouraged me to write my first two books, both published in 1976—*Television: A Guide for Christians* and *Gadgets, Gimmicks, and Grace: A Handbook on Multimedia in Church and School*. The first came about when a book editor read my *Christian Century* article "The Gospel According to Edith Bunker." We both thought this could be expanded into a book on the theology in the popular TV series *All in the Family*. Such was not to be—another Presbyterian pastor beat me to the punch by a few weeks. (Spencer Marsh's book *God, Man & Archie Bunker* was so good that I used it and its accompanying tape cassette with both adult and confirmation classes. My consolation prize was in hearing Henry Fonda, narrating the TV special "The 100th Broadcast of *All in the Family*," read a quotation from my Edith Bunker article, giving me credit before an audience of fifty million!) The second book led to my becoming a film and television reviewer for the Catholic order that published the family magazine *Marriage & Family Living*, as well as such books as mine.

During the '70s and '80s I wrote for various other journals: *Group Magazine; Religion Teachers Journal; Today's Parish; Christian Herald*; and *Mass Media Newsletter*. The latter included reviews of theatrical films by others, my contributions being a "how to" column on multimedia, reviews of short films, and study guides for the films that *MMN* rented and sold. When *MMN* was sold to a Catholic publisher, I became the editor. However, unable to generate enough revenue, it folded, leaving a gap in the church publication field.

In 1990, equipped with a $50 check from a speaking engagement (about film and the church, of course), I persuaded my presbytery to sponsor a monthly film newsletter for pastors and educators. I was chair of the presbytery media committee, and so had some official standing. What triggered my long-held desire to do this was the appearance in quick succession of four films that I thought church leaders should see: *Driving Miss Daisy, Glory, Born on the Fourth of July*, and *Crimes and Misdemeanors*. These seemed like an auspicious configuration of excellent films to write about. I called the newsletter by a name which I thought others might recognize—*Visual Parables*—the name, as mentioned earlier, under which I had sent out so many multimedia presentations in kit form to churches during the two decades before. The first issue was a one-sheet, two-sided publication, so the reviews were short. As the readership spread beyond the presbytery, the newsletter grew to four pages, and then to six, counting the film guide inserted. Over the years, when others took over the publishing chores, *VP* became a magazine, for a while even graced by a color cover. One of the features added was a devotional column entitled "Praying the Movies." This proved to be popular with readers, and eventually resulted in the first edition of *Praying the Movies* from Geneva Press (sibling imprint to Westminster John Knox Press).

When *VP* was launched, I was serving a Dayton, Ohio, inner-city church and working on a doctor of ministry degree in art, film, and theology. During my first month in town I was featured in local newscasts on all three network affiliates, quoted in the area newspapers, and invited to speak on a radio talk show. The reason for this attention was that a colleague spread the word to the media that I had read and liked the novel on which a forthcoming film, *The Last Temptation of Christ*, was based. It was an exciting time, with me walking through a crowd, estimated by the police to number over 450, who were protesting the opening of the film at the downtown Neon Movies. A priest, momentarily famous like myself (his fifteen minutes of fame arose from his banning a parishioner from church because the latter insisted on wearing shorts to mass), was encircling the theater while sprinkling holy water, allegedly to dispel evil spirits attached to the "blasphemous" film. All of us who entered the theater had to pass through a metal detector because of bomb threats. We might say, "It's only a movie," but the incident showed me what passions a film can arouse! It also showed that if a church leader would speak an appreciative word in support of a notable film, the world would take notice.

The Neon's proprietor appreciated my defending his right to show the films and, once I had seen it, the movie itself (despite its flaws). This helped make him open to a proposal for a church-sponsored film series on six Sunday afternoons. Thus was born the Lenten Film Series, which lasted some ten years (including three years after I had left the city). It was sponsored by Dayton's equivalent of the Council of Churches and was financially supported by donations from a number of Catholic and Protestant congregations. Drawing many non-churched young adults, as well as church members, the film showings provided a forum for discussion of issues and concerns, our discussions held right in the theater. During the year that our series dealt with important social issues, we invited local leaders to help lead the discussions—such as the director of the local shelter after *The Saint of Fort Washington*; an AIDS leader and an HIV-positive client following *Philadelphia*; and a Holocaust survivor after *Schindler's List*.[1]

Not every church can sponsor a film series for the public, but any church can at least start a small film discussion group. As few as four people can still gain a lot from watching and discussing a film together. I have enjoyed working with such groups in every church that I have served, learning much myself from the process. Sometimes we met in homes, thus avoiding the problem of copyright infringement (more on that at the end of this Introduction). Sometimes we went to a movie theater and then held the discussion in a home. When

1. Anyone interested in setting up such a series is encouraged to read my paper "The Church and Theater." Send two first-class stamps and a self-addressed envelope to Edward McNulty, 63 Boone Lake, Walton, KY 41094.

videos were introduced, we often watched the film on a home monitor. Refreshments helped lubricate the discussion and create a relaxed atmosphere (as opposed to watching the film in a church classroom). The advantages of seeing a film at the theater are, of course, viewing the film as intended, on a big screen with sound that surrounds you, whereas a video allows you to choose any old or recent film and show it according to your schedule. A good compromise is to show a video via a video projector onto a large screen or wall. Even though video projectors are still very expensive, this is not beyond the means of a small church. Many church and school offices have projectors that can be borrowed or rented.

When I pastored a 100-member church in upstate New York, we were able, through a grant from our presbytery and from a local foundation, to purchase a video projector and a 12-foot fold-up screen. On a Saturday night we turned our local public library into a movie theater. When we opened the movies to the public, we had to change the name from "God and the Movies" to "Movies That Matter" because the village atheist, who loved movies as much as I, started coming. With an ecumenical mixture of Christians and Jews we had some delightful, lively discussions. Our series even drew one or two film folks from New York City who "weekended" in the area. A highlight of the series for everyone was when Broadway actress Cherry Jones demonstrated to our group some of the ways she clung to the rope of the capsized boat in *The Perfect Storm*, or how she spoke on the telephone from her Manhattan apartment while talking with Kristin Scott Thomas, who at that very moment was being filmed by Robert Redford as part of a scene (from *The Horse Whisperer*) in which she is talking with her veterinarian (played by Jones).

As with the Dayton Lenten Series, we found that a good film provides an excellent means of bringing people together to deal with important issues of life. As I look back on my life and ministry I can, from this vantage point, discern the hand of God bringing together a lonely boy, life-enhancing films, and the caring ministry of the church with unexpected results. The most rewarding compliment I keep receiving after one of my workshops or articles is a variation of "Thank you. I now look at films in a new way." I still look forward to the unfolding of a new film as an invitation to set forth on a journey of discovery, one that sometimes enriches the spirit as well as the imagination.

Using This Book

In my work I have utilized two basic approaches to using film—the didactic/analytical approach and the spiritual or devotional approach. Both are helpful and enjoyable. The first uses one's critical tools to analyze how the film is put together, what its themes are, what the motivations of the characters are, and much more. I use this approach in my *Films and Faith* book and in the reviews I write for *Visual Parables*. It is also the basis for most of the books being written about film and theology.

The second approach is the basis for this book. Although critical faculties are still needed, lest we be led down wrong paths by an inferior film, here we are seeking that elusive moment, referred to by an Asian theologian as an "Aha!" moment, when the Spirit awakens us to something special in the film. It may be an act of one of the characters, a word, a song, an image, or the way all the elements of a shot or scene come together in the perfect way, making us aware that we are on holy ground.

In the first edition of *Praying the Movies* I described how, after reading the first of Malcolm Boyd's film meditations, in *Are You Running With Me, Jesus?* I began thinking about this idea, and how, while watching Zeffirelli's critically panned *Brother Sun, Sister Moon*, I felt a closeness of the Holy Spirit and the spirit of Francis of Assisi. (See the Introduction in my earlier book for a fuller description of this experience and of the text of Father Boyd's meditation. Also, note that a new edition of his classic book has recently been published.) Each of the thirty-one films in this collection, as well as the first one, have provided such an encounter for me, and I hope they will for any who read this book.

When I wrote the devotionals for the first collection, I envisioned the book as being a resource for an individual or a small group wanting devotional material that was a little off the beaten track. Apparently it met that goal: a film director told me he kept the book near his bed, and a producer, with whom I was talking on the telephone, asked if I were the same McNulty who wrote the book he had used for his devotions that morning. Best of all was an e-mail from a reader in England who sent thanks for the book, saying that it helped him at a time when he was having difficulty in hearing God "through the traditional disciplines" of the church. (Such a message makes an author's whole week, not just one day!) I still see this use by individuals as primary, though a couple of pastors have said that they built worship services around some of the devotionals, adding, of course, more prayers and hymns according to their liturgical custom.

As before, there are thirty-one meditations, one for each day of a long month. There are passages from both the Hebrew and the Christian Scriptures that form the foundation for the reflections about the film scene(s). Sometimes I deal with these in the reflection sections; often I do not, leaving it up to readers to make the connections. You can be assured that there are such, as I spent many hours with various Bible study aids to find suitable passages. I hope there is more exegesis than eisegesis in the selections—also that every Christian home will have a hymnal, so that even if readers are using the book for private devotions, they can read or sing the words to the hymns I've suggested. Like the carefully selected songs on a movie soundtrack, these hymns offer a variation of the theme of the film and Scripture passages. They are integral to the devotional, and not just decorative. The concluding prayer is for those times when words come hard: readers may use them as is, or as a launching pad for their own prayer.

When using the book in a group, the leader should take seriously the caution notes for some of the films. Not everyone can tolerate the elements of an R-rated film. This problem can be easily handled if the leader is describing the film scene, but might prove difficult if showing the actual clip. Double the caution if you want to use the clip in a public worship service. One of the reasons I moved "God and the Movies" from our homes and then our church building when the group grew too large was that I did not believe it wise to show such films as *The Fisher King* or *American History X* in the sanctuary. I tried to select movie scenes with little or no offensive elements, but sometimes I believe it was the Spirit, and not I, choosing the scene in order to impart some new insight or call to action.

Group leaders can involve more people if they assign members to read the Scripture passages and read or give the prayer. If the group will not be singing the hymn, another member could, and should, read the words. In using the earlier book, some who use the video scene itself said that it was time consuming to find the scene I had described—a valid criticism. Therefore this time I have provided cues to find the scene. For VHS tapes I start timing from the moment the studio logo appears on the screen. (Because of variations among VHS players, the minutes and seconds are approximations.) DVD counters are more accurate, so as often as possible, I used the DVD version of a film in giving the beginning and stopping times. The numbers, from left to right, are the hour, minutes, and seconds from the beginning of the film. Leaders planning to use a tape should have it cued up and ready to go so that technical details will not be distracting.

The meditations can be used at the beginning or the end of a class in which a similar theme is being explored. Lots of leaders have used the meditations to enrich a retreat. The subject might not be film study but rather a theme to which a film might relate. Six times I have participated in the Presbyterian Peacemaking conferences by teaching a workshop on films related to racism, human rights, children, or whatever the conference theme is. I have never had any difficulty in finding films that explore or enhance our understanding of the theme or issue.

A Further Word About R-Rated Films

Most young adults have few problems with viewing R-rated films. They reject the old "garbage in, garbage out" argument of those who regard Hollywood as the cause of so many societal ills. They know that people should be able to discern the good from the bad, and thus not be afraid of being tainted by those elements of a film of which they do not approve. Not everyone is of this mind, however. Each year after *Presbyterians Today* publishes my Top Ten Films article, I can expect some letters protesting the inclusion of R-rated films. If you are one who is uncomfortable with swear words and scenes of violence and sex in a film, what follows is for you.

I can sympathize with the protesters, being myself such a person who dislikes the street language, graphic violence, and sex of many films. However, two arguments keep me watching. The first involves the intent of the filmmakers: Are they approving of the action, such as the violence? Or are they showing how destructive to human relationships it can be? Or are they maybe even making fun of it, laughter often being the best way of dealing with some things? The violence of a movie like *Dirty Harry* is very different from that of a film like *Saving Private Ryan* or, to use one of Clint Eastwood's most perceptive films, *Unforgiven*. Movies like *Dirty Harry* not only approve of violence as being the best way of dealing with evil persons, but also show it as being fun. In a sequel, Harry says to a fallen crook looking at his gun a few inches away, "Go ahead, make my day." He can hardly wait for the bad guy to give him a reason for blasting away. A president quoted the film, sadly for some of us, with approval. *Private Ryan* or *The Three Kings*, being war movies, display a lot more violence than *Dirty Harry*, but the filmmakers' obvious purpose is to show how horrible war is and what guns and bullets do to human bodies—very different from those old John Wayne films when we kids could scarcely wait to see him killing "Japs" or "savage Injuns."

The language of several of the characters in John Singleton's *Boyz N the Hood* was terrible, as was the violence, but the filmmaker was showing us what it is like to be a young man in the black ghetto, something that no white person can experience except through such an honest film as this one. The main character comes to reject the violence of his friends, finally seeing the wisdom of his father, something that many who rejected the film overlooked.

The second reason I keep watching is religiously based. I see certain films as visual parables, "earthen vessels" containing the treasure of the gospel. I was intrigued forty years ago when I read an article by the Jesuit Fr. John Culkin in which he claimed that Jesus the parablemaker would become Jesus the filmmaker were he to return to earth today in his mission of reaching the people. A parable is not the simple illustration Jesus used in making a point, as too many of us were mistaught in Sunday school. When we look at the three Synoptic Gospels, we see that instead of enlightening, his parables often confused and at times maybe even upset his listeners by challenging their accepted prejudices. When asked by a lawyer, "Who is my neighbor?" Jesus' response was the parable of the Good Samaritan, an oxymoron to most Jews of the time who hated this people. It was not the religious leaders, the priest and the Levite, who helped the injured man, but a member of a despised ethnic group who took care of him. Or, in his story about the Pharisee and the hated tax collector, it is not the pious Pharisee who is the hero, but the man regarded as a collaborator with the Roman occupiers, the tax collector. Today such a film as *Philadelphia* challenges our views of and way of treating homosexuals, and even such children's films as *Babe: Pig in the City* or *The Iron Giant* call into question our accepted, violent responses to enemies.

In his First Letter to the Corinthians, the apostle Paul defends himself from his enemies' charge that he is such an imperfect man that he is unfit to preach the gospel. Paul says that he is like an earthen vessel that contains the treasure of the gospel. Some R-rated films are like that, containing scenes of love and sacrifice, beauty and nobility, that lift our spirits, despite some of the words and actions of the characters. To dismiss such films out of hand would be to miss out on real treasures. Furthermore, many of the people whom Jesus associated with were R-rated, and in a few cases, even X-rated (or should we say, in the light of the revision of the Motion Picture Code, NC-17-rated?). Jesus did not turn away from them, even though he was criticized by those overly worried about his association with such unworthies ("Garbage in, garbage out"). True, he did not approve of Zacchaeus's thievery or of what the woman caught in adultery did in the dark, but he did not reject them. Nor should we do so with a film that has some elements of which we disapprove yet teaches that violence accomplishes nothing lasting or that justice and truth will prevail despite the forces arrayed against them.

Something that George F. McLeod wrote many years ago in *Only One Way Left*, his book urging the church to become involved in solving social injustices, applies here also. It once was a favorite quotation of writers and preachers, so it deserves to be revisited:

> I simply argue that the Cross be raised again at the center of the market-place as well as on the steeple of the church. I am recovering the claim that Jesus was not crucified in a cathedral

between two candles, but on a cross between two thieves; on the town garbage-heap; at a crossroad so cosmopolitan that they had to write his title in Hebrew and in Latin and in Greek (or shall we say in English, in Bantu and in Afrikaans?); at the kind of place where cynics talk smut, and thieves curse, and soldiers gamble. Because this is where He died. And that is what He died about. And that is where churchmen should be and what churchmanship should be about.[2]

Indeed it is. And that is why churchmen and churchwomen should not turn away from the movie theater. Our faith must not be the sheltered, hothouse variety, but strong enough to take whatever the filmmaker serves up to us—as long as that earthen vessel of a film contains some nugget of the gospel.

Staying Legal and Ethical

We all have seen that threatening note from the FBI at the beginning of every videotape and DVD. Home video products are created for the home and not for public consumption. Many church leaders, however, ignore the warning and show a video picked up at a video store or library. Most churches will get away with it—although some film studios are now sending people out to look through newspapers and such to ferret out offending churches and prosecute them. But aside from the illegality of showing a film without a license

2. *Only One Way Left*, 3d ed. (Glasgow, Iona, Edinburgh: The Iona Community, 1961), 38.

or permission, there is the ethical issue of using someone's work without paying them for it.

There is an easy way to fulfill both the legal and the ethical requirements for showing a film at church, and that is to obtain a yearly license from the Motion Picture Licensing Corporation (MPLC). The cost for the annual license will depend on the size of the church and other factors. It might range from $100 for a small congregation to $200 or so for larger ones. Sponsoring groups cannot charge an admission fee for a film, but they can leave an offering plate for donations. We found that this gathered in enough money to pay for the license, as well as meeting the cost of a bulb replacement (no small matter for a video projector!) or the purchase of a few videos. The MPLC does not include every film studio, but you will find most of them on its extensive list. For detailed information contact the MPLC by one of the following means:

Motion Picture Licensing Corporation,
5455 Centinela Ave., Los Angeles, CA 90066.
Phone: 1-800-462-8855
On-line: http://www.mplc.com

Here's to film viewing that is inspirational—and legal.

1. *American Beauty*
Celebrating the Ordinary

For God speaks in one way,
and in two, though people do not perceive it.
In a dream, in a vision of the night,
when deep sleep falls on mortals,
while they slumber on their beds. . . .

Job 33:14–15

The heavens are telling the glory of God;
and the firmament proclaims his handiwork.
Day to day pours forth speech,
and night to night declares knowledge.
There is no speech, nor are there words;
their voice is not heard;
yet their voice goes out through all the earth,
and their words to the end of the world.

Psalm 19:1–4

For what can be known about God is plain to
them, because God has shown it to them. Ever
since the creation of the world his eternal power
and divine nature, invisible though they are, have
been understood and seen through the things he
has made.

Romans 1:19–20a

Introduction

Back in the heyday of posters some thirty years ago,
one of my favorite wall decorations was based on a
quotation from the philosopher John Dewey: "Art is
the celebration of the ordinary." Those days were the
highpoint of the influence of Corita Kent, a Catholic
nun turned professional artist, whose colorful poster

art combined quotations of pop songwriters and advertising slogans with passages from the Bible and theologians. She and Dewey kept me on my toes looking for manifestations of beauty and the divine in my urban and suburban environment, such as on billboards or in the colorful ads of magazines. There is a scene in the five-time Academy Award winner *American Beauty* that brought back memories of those days and the never-forgotten insights gleaned even from posters and advertisements.

American Beauty in many ways is a strange film, beginning as a satire on suburban life and values, but then veering off to explore the depths of human longing and desperation. It is as if Flannery O'Connor had made a film, with the anti-hero Lester Burnham lusting after the classmate of his teenaged daughter, and then coming to his senses just in time, finally breaking through to an awareness of the spiritual beauty and nature of the universe just as his life ends. However, before Lester's epiphany there is another one. It too comes to an unlikely candidate for spiritual insight—Ricky, a teenager who earns money to buy his expensive video and electronic equipment from the sale of drugs. The boy, living next door to the Burnhams, has become infatuated with Lester's surly daughter Jane. Ricky, always carrying his camcorder, trains it on Jane at school and when they are at home. Jane's bedroom faces his, so he watches for her at night so that he can capture her image on tape. Jane is upset by this unwelcome attention from someone she considers beneath her, but slowly Ricky's persistence in refusing to be put off by her snubs wins her over. In the scene that follows he invites her home after school.

The Scene

Time into film: 1:01:45   Stop at 1:04:52

Ricky introduces Jane to his almost catatonic mother and then leads her into his military father's study. After showing Jane the Nazi plate so prized by his father, he asks, "What's wrong?" Although she replies, "Nothing," he can see that she is afraid of him. He looks at her for a few moments, then asks if she wants to see something beautiful. The scene takes place in his bedroom as they sit before a TV monitor. The image is outdoors, where we see an ordinary, empty plastic bag blowing in the wind. The wind whips the bag about in circles, raises it high above the ground, and then downward, the bag twisting and turning, almost as if it had a life of its own and is dancing to a song of the universe that only it can hear.

As they sit on his bed raptly looking at the scene, Ricky explains that it was a winter day when it was close to snowing. Sensing an electricity in the air, he describes the bag like it was a little kid dancing with him, begging him to play. For fifteen minutes he watched and taped it, as he came to realize that there was a Life behind things, "this incredibly benevolent force that wanted me to know there was no reason to be afraid. Ever." He knows, he tells her, that his video is a pale reflection of the actual experience, but it helps him to remember. "I need to remember," he adds.

Now Jane is watching him instead of the screen, as he continues, "Sometimes there's so much beauty in the world I feel like I can't take it . . . and my heart is going to cave in." Jane takes his hand, and then, leaning over, kisses him softly on the lips. Ricky gazes lovingly at her, but then the mood is broken as Jane, sensing the lateness of the hour, asks what time it is and dashes home, late for dinner.

Reflection on the Scene

It might seem odd to some that such an epiphany revealing the spiritual side and the beauty of the universe should be given to a teenager dealing drugs to his classmates, but then those who know their Scriptures are aware that the Creator of the universe often revealed himself to, and used, such unsavory persons as the conniving Jacob or Rahab the harlot. Equally surprising to others is the fact that Ricky saw such beauty and spiritual meaning in a castaway plastic bag, something in which we carry home our merchandise and groceries and then throw away by the millions. Most people would have passed it by without a glance. If they had given it even a moment's thought, they might have been upset that someone had littered the yard. But not Ricky. His eyes see more than just a plastic bag. It is transformed in his mind and soul into a child-like cosmic dancer, inviting him to join with the universe in a dance of life. He is but a breath away from discovering the one whom the church has called the Lord of the Dance.

Ricky sorely needs such an epiphany. The son of a harsh father who is unsure of his own sexuality and fearful of anyone or anything outside of the narrow universe bounded by his military lifestyle, Ricky has seen his mother reduced by her spouse to an almost dead person unable to see any beauty or experience anything of the joy of the universe. He has rebelled against his father's regimen and seems headed in the wrong direction, but we can hope that his love for Jane and his new-found revelation will spread through his life, sending him in a more wholesome direction.

Ricky has learned what even the false comforter Elihu knew when he tried to convince Job that his suffering came as a warning from God—that God "speaks in one way, and in two, though people do not perceive it." To the pious, "The heavens are telling the glory of God," whereas to the more earthbound Rickys, living in cities where the night lights blot out the stars, it might be more mundane things like plastic bags blowing in the wind or even, as Corita Kent led me to see, a billboard selling beer with the slogan, "Serve and Enjoy." (I took a slide of that slogan and used it in presentations on Christ's call to us to follow him.) Ricky would like what poet Elizabeth Barrett Browning wrote long ago (which also appeared on a poster in the 1960s and '70s):

Earth's crammed with heaven
And every common bush afire with God;
And only he who sees takes off his shoes—
The rest sit round it and pluck blackberries.

Ricky, as one who has "eyes that see," has indeed removed his shoes and invites Jane to do likewise. He has a long way to go in his moral life, but he is well on his way to discovering what the apostle Paul was conveying about God to the Christians at Rome.

For Further Reflection

1. Where or how have you seen God, or something spiritual, in the ordinary? What have you saved that helps you remember such a special occasion?

2. Why do you think we do not have such experiences more often? Is it because we are not looking or expecting much?

3. It is the contention of these movie devotions that this experience can happen in a movie theater as well as in a church sanctuary. When has your movie experience become a spiritual one, lifting you beyond the realm of entertainment?

4. How can you share this insight with others or help them develop eyes that see?

HYMN: "Open My Eyes That I Might See"

A Prayer

Gracious and ever-creating God, you have created us in your image and called us to be creative in our own lives. We thank you for the creative, challenging works of artists and filmmakers like Sam Mendes. Help us to see your world through their child-like eyes, so similar to those of Christ, that we might see in even the wind-tossed trash of our world a revelation of your divine presence. In stars and atoms, in flowers and weeds, in that which is held as precious, and in that which is discarded as worthless, may we see your loving, caressing hand. We ask this in the name of your Son Jesus Christ, who took such pleasure in the ordinary people of his time. Amen.

2. *Babe*
An Unprejudiced Heart

Partiality in judging is not good.

Proverbs 24:23

Then Peter began to speak to them: "I truly understand that God shows no partiality, but in

every nation anyone who fears him and does
what is right is acceptable to him.

Acts 10:34–35

From now on, therefore, we regard no one from
a human point of view; even though we once
knew Christ from a human point of view, we
know him no longer in that way. So if anyone is
in Christ, there is a new creation: everything old
has passed away; see, everything has become new!

2 Corinthians 5:16–17

Introduction

Although there are still adults who have not seen *Babe*
because they mistakenly think that it is "just a children's film," many more have discovered that both the
humor and the insights into relationships make it a
film literally for children of all ages. Introduced in the
narration as a fable about a little pig "with an unprejudiced heart," it is the story of how one person (or creature) can make a difference in a world that accepts too
easily "the way that things are."

When Farmer Hoggett wins the little pig in a lot-
tery at the fair, he names it Babe and takes him home,
where sheep dog Fly kindly takes the pig into her family of pups. Her gruff mate Rex would prefer not to
mix creatures, but he reluctantly goes along with her,
keeping the pig at a distance. Babe learns that on the
farm there are strict boundaries to be observed; pigs
definitely are not allowed in Farmer Hoggett's house,
nor allowed to go with the dogs when they are led out
to herd the sheep. The latter, Babe has been told, are
"stupid," requiring the firm guidance of man and dog
for survival.

The Scene

Time into film: 0:11:58   Stop at 0:14:35

Just after being left behind by Fly and her family, Babe discovers another side, a darker one, to life on the farm. Attracted by the sound of moaning and coughing coming from a shed, Babe goes to the door and calls to the creature. It replies "Darn wolf!" and Babe replies that he is not a wolf. "What are you?" he asks. "A ewe," comes the reply. Mistaking the answer, Babe again asks, "What are you?" When Babe calls it a sheep, the ewe proudly and pointedly responds that she is not "a common sheep," but a ewe, a mature female sheep. She introduces herself as Maa. When she sees how polite Babe is, she tells him that he is not at all like those "wolves" who "treat you like dirt." She describes the dogs as mean and vicious, savages, some of them so bad that they "run a sheep down and tear it to pieces." Babe protests that Fly would never do that, and Maa responds, "A right vicious creature is she." The old ewe says that such "a gentle soul" as Babe should not be mixing with such company.

It is a troubled little pig who returns to his bed in the barn. Cruel? Vicious? He had never seen Fly act that way! Questions about what the dogs do in the fields all day plague him until, at the end of the day, Farmer Hoggett's wagon, with Fly riding in the back, returns to the farmyard. Fly licks him in a motherly fashion. Surely the old sheep was wrong, Babe thinks, and promises himself that he will never think badly of another creature.

Reflection on the Scene

Babe has discovered what most children learn sooner or later, that society entertains certain stereotypes.

Dogs are "wolves" to the sheep, mean and vicious. And in turn, the sheep dogs inform Babe that sheep are all "stupid." Such stereotypes determine the way members of the two groups relate to one another: the sheep shun contact with "wolves"; the sheep dogs, convinced of the stupidity of the sheep, use fear, and sometimes actual violence, to make the sheep do what Farmer Hoggett wants them to do. And now Babe has come upon creatures who do not fit the stereotype. He finds that Maa is actually a wise old creature, perfectly capable of rational thought and communication, definitely not "stupid." And no one has treated Babe more kindly than has Fly, so he knows that "wolf" is not a proper label for her. This knowledge of the falseness of stereotypes will lead the little Babe to challenge the rule of stereotypes, "changing forever," the narrator says, "our valley."

Babe, of course, is a fable, and real-life sheep are not the most intelligent of creatures, and even the most domesticated of dogs still have the ways of the hunter as a part of their nature. But the fable does remind us and our children that prejudice can reside in human hearts and the inferior stereotypes we accept can blind us to the true nature of members of other groups. "Jews have no dealings with Samaritans," John informs his readers. Centuries later that was translated to "Whites have no dealings with coloreds—except as master and slave." "Coloreds"—and far worse labels have been used—were seen by whites as slow of wit and speech, instinctively rhythmic, lazy, yet overly sexed and eager to copulate with white women—clearly in need of a firm (read "white") hand for guidance and control. Such a view was fed to most whites and blacks along with their mother's milk until it became accepted by both groups as "the way things are." Those who challenge a system built on prejudice usually pay a stiff price: ostracism, persecution, and even death.

Similar prejudices are taught to us about other groups. Women are the "weaker sex," ruled by their emotions and incapable of sustained serious thought; they therefore must be "kept in their place," namely, the kitchen or the home. Homosexuals are limp-wristed, sick creatures, promiscuous or, worse, eager to seduce our children; they are therefore to be despised and rooted out of "normal" society. Jews are rich money-grubbers. Arabs are either bomb-making terrorists or oil-rich sheiks. Catholics are. . . . Protestants are. . . . And the lists go on and on, separating the ins from the outs, the desirables from the undesirables, the superior from the inferior.

In the fable, little Babe, the one "with an unprejudiced heart," begins to question the stereotypes and thus the system of how the groups should relate to one another. Babe is like Jesus in this regard. A Jew with "an unprejudiced heart," Jesus ignored the dictum that "Jews have no dealings with Samaritans" and freely mingled with them. He challenged the barriers raised by Jewish prejudice and made a Samaritan the hero of his famous parable—the good neighbor who stopped to help the mugged man was not a Jewish leader who "passed by on the other side," but a despised Samaritan. Jesus also challenged the traditional, patriarchal views about women, most notably in his acceptance of Mary as a student during his visit—much to the dismay of her sister Martha, who apparently did not see beyond her role as server of the needs of men. Later on, through a dream, the apostle Peter was led to see that the once despised Gentiles were as acceptable to Christ as Jews. At about the same time, Saul of

Tarsus was captive to the old prejudices, even persecuting those who taught differently, until his encounter with the risen Christ changed his heart forever. That same risen Christ continues to confront us, transforming our hearts so that we can no longer entertain the old stereotypes of "wolves," "stupid sheep," "coloreds," and all the rest. Indeed, we join with St. Paul in affirming, "From now on, therefore, we regard no one from a human point of view; even though we once knew Christ from a human point of view, we know him no longer in that way. So if anyone is in Christ, there is a new creation: everything old has passed away; see, everything has become new!"

For Further Reflection

1. What stereotype, based on long-held prejudice, have you been taught? How did it determine your feelings toward and your relationship with members of the other group? Have you had experiences similar to Babe's that challenged the stereotype? How did you feel about the challenge? What, if any, changes has it led you to make in your life?

2. Old prejudices and stereotypes die hard: how do they still recur? How do you struggle against them? What have you found that helps you in the struggle? Prayer? Association with others who are "recovering racists"—such as in church or groups dedicated to combating prejudice and fostering justice and brother/sisterhood? Other?

3. How does Christ (or if you are not a Christian, some other guiding principle) make a difference when you are confronted with a stereotype, such as when your friends or associates at work repeat an ethnic joke

in which members of "inferior" groups are stereotyped and put down?

4. How are you preparing any children in your life to have "unprejudiced hearts"? What other prejudice-combating stories and videos, in addition to *Babe*, have you encountered that can be used with children?

A Prayer

"Create in me a clean heart, O God, and put a new and right spirit within me": Like the psalmist, may we purge away all the prejudices and harsh judgments of those who do not know you. Give us the mind of Christ so that we might wage the good fight in a world still ruled by ancient prejudices. And when you give us small victories over prejudice, save us from smug complacency that we have triumphed or that we are superior to those still enslaved by false images of others. Help us to continue the outer battle against all racist or stereotypical practices that separate us and confine us to "proper" roles or places in life. May we believe and act on the faith that you have made us "of one blood" and desire us to live together in loving, compassionate ways. We pray this in the name of the One in whom there is "neither Greek nor Jew, neither male nor female, slave nor free," even Jesus Christ, our Lord. Amen.

3. *Beyond Rangoon*
An Inspirational Role Model

> But Moses said to the people, "Do not be afraid, stand firm and see the deliverance that the Lord will accomplish for you today. . . ."
>
> Exodus 14:13a

After he had washed their feet, had put on his robe, and had returned to the table, he said to them, "Do you know what I have done to you? You call me Teacher and Lord—and you are right, for that is what I am. So if I, your Lord and Teacher, have washed your feet, you also ought to wash one another's feet. For I have set you an example, that you also should do as I have done to you."

John 13:12–15

As an example of suffering and patience, beloved, take the prophets who spoke in the name of the Lord. Indeed we call blessed those who showed endurance. You have heard of the endurance of Job, and you have seen the purpose of the Lord, how the Lord is compassionate and merciful.

James 5:10-11

Beloved, do not imitate what is evil but imitate what is good. Whoever does good is from God; whoever does evil has not seen God.

3 John 11

Introduction

Although it has not won the critical acclaim that *Hope and Glory* has, I have long appreciated John Boorman's *Beyond Rangoon* and have indeed drawn from it several times when speaking or writing about grief and role models. Set in the exotic country of Burma, where a military clique keeps the people in subjugation by the use of terror and force, it is the story of a young woman's journey from despair and inertia to a state of hope and useful activity. Laura Bowman is a young doctor not able to practice medicine any more. She has not been able to recover from the trauma of the murder of her husband and child one night while she was away. Filled with guilt, remorse, and grief, she has withdrawn into herself. Her sister takes her in tow and brings her on a group tour of Southeast Asia in the hope of awakening in Laura some interest in life. But Laura almost sleepwalks her way with the group as they visit the exotic tourist sites. She seems oblivious to the fascinating beauty around her. When Laura freaks out after seeing a little boy fall from a giant statue, even her sister comes to believe that the trip is a mistake. But events of that night will make them both change their minds, though in very different ways.

The Scene

Time into film: 0:8:40   Stop at 0:13:40

Laura does not sleep well during the last night of their stay in Rangoon. She cannot keep her torturous past from invading her dreams. When she hears the distant noise of a crowd, she gets up to try to discover what is happening. She sees nothing other than the darkened streets, but hearing the continuing noise, she dresses and leaves her room. It is curfew hour, a time when everyone is forbidden by the dictators to be abroad, but Laura ventures into the street anyway. Still not seeing anything, she heads toward the direction of the crowd noise. She passes by a group of soldiers standing back in the shadows, their rifles equipped with bayonets, but she pays them no heed. She seems driven by the urge to investigate the source of the sound disturbing the stillness of the night.

She comes out onto a square and discovers a large crowd standing around as if they are waiting for something—or someone. In the distance she spies a large procession of people moving toward the square. There is the sound of commands given, and, accompanied by the harsh thud of boots upon the pavement, the unit of soldiers she has just passed rush into the square. They form a line blocking off the oncoming procession and those awaiting them. A young Burmese woman asks in English if Laura is an American. Wanting to share what for her is to be a special moment, she invites Laura to climb up onto a stone platform with her for a better look. She tells Laura that she and the others are waiting for Aung San Suu Kyi. When Laura indicates that she does not know who she is, the young woman tells her that Aung San Suu Kyi is the leader of the democratic struggle against the generals in Burma. She is very brave, she tells her.

Just *how* brave we see in the following moments. The camera shows us a beautiful woman dressed in white, marching at the head of the procession. Flanked by her aides, she seems the picture of serenity amidst all the turmoil surrounding her. She and her followers stop when the army officer harshly orders them to halt. After a moment's pause, Aung San Suu Kyi moves again toward the soldiers. She brushes off a nervous assistant who would hold her back, nodding to him that it is all right.

The line of soldiers stand with their rifles pointed directly at Aung San Suu Kyi. The officer continues to bark out his order for her to stop, but she keeps on approaching the line. She places her hands together in the Eastern gesture for peace and respect. Her face is calm, with the trace of a smile. The soldiers are obviously unnerved by her fearless advance. They have the guns, but she seems to have the power. One of them shakes visibly, his finger still on the trigger. Laura, her new friend, and all the onlookers hold their breath, the suspense thicker than fog. Aung San Suu Kyi walks right up to the shaking soldier, gently sweeps his gun aside, and strolls through the line. She ascends the speakers' platform and waves to her supporters. They break into a joyous cheer, the soldiers standing by, irrelevant because of their powerlessness.

Laura has been transfixed by the sight of the courage of the Burmese leader, a woman whom until this night she had not even known about. Her face is suffused with a light that had gone out of her, returning now only because of the example of another woman facing a similar darkness and possessed with the faith and the courage to overcome it.

Reflection on the Scene

The story of Laura is fictional, but the character of Aung San Suu Kyi is not. In Burma she has stood against the dictators like a rock. Even though banned from public speaking and held under house arrest, her presence in the country has become a powerful witness against oppression. She once led her party to the polls in opposition to the generals. In fact, she won the election, but the military refused to accept the verdict of the people. Had she not won the Nobel Peace Prize, and the notoriety that goes with the prize, Aung San Suu Kyi probably would have been imprisoned or killed. She has paid a great price, unable to join her ailing husband in England during the illness that led to his death. Nor has she been able to see her son, now a teenager, for many years. Possessing no guns or army, Aung San Suu Kyi is nonetheless a power to contend with.

Thus her effect on Laura Bowman in the film is perfectly believable. Laura entered that square out of curiosity and with a need to find something that would stir her deep down. She leaves the square deeply moved by the example of a woman unafraid to die. She would not have been able to understand Aung San Suu Kyi's speech, but the leader's example of courageously facing down the armed soldiers needed no translation.

The encounter becomes the defining moment for the rest of Laura's life. Forced to drop out of the tourist group because she has lost her passport during the night, Laura is left alone in Rangoon until she can obtain a new one. Wanting to see more of the country and its people, she becomes involved with a guide who takes her, at her request, "beyond Rangoon." She discovers how desperate the people are under the oppressive rule of the military. Learning that her guide is a former professor banned for his political activities, she becomes involved with some of his students, and then is forced to flee into the jungle because soldiers are seeking them out. Their lives at risk, Laura's long-dormant medical skills are now greatly needed. Submerging her own needs by serving the greater needs of others, she finds health and wholeness for herself. Like the courageous woman who stared down the armed soldiers in the square, Laura has found a purpose in life greater than her personal loss and is thus able to overcome her grief.

We all need someone to look up to, especially when we are young or, as in Laura's case, troubled and confused—someone who provides us with the clues and the inspiration for coping with a difficult situation. Today we call such persons role models. Although the term itself is not used in the Scriptures, the word "example" is. Christ sets the example for the kind of life his followers are called to lead when he strips down and washes their feet. The epistle writers refer to him as the supreme example, and the apostle Paul invites his readers to regard his own life as an example, insofar as they see him following Christ.

If we have been fortunate, we carry the memory of numerous people who have provided us with an example of how to live—parents or other relatives, a teacher at church or school, a pastor, or a kindly neighbor. Some of us are old enough to recall that there was a time when we found heroes in the political realm, a Roosevelt, Eisenhower, Kennedy, or Stevenson. Few would look for a role model among politicians today, thanks to the cynical, debunking press and the sleazy deeds of the politicians themselves. The media, of course, is always invading our consciousness, serving us up sports and entertainment figures to imitate. Part of our maturing process involves our sorting out those who are merely celebrities, and often unruly, self-centered ones at that, from those persons truly worth emulating, such as Aung San Suu Kyi.

For Further Reflection

1. As you reflect back on your life, who has served as a role model? Someone touted by the media, such as a rock or movie star? Have you always had the same role models, or did you adopt new ones as you grew older?

2. Have you trusted perhaps too much in a role model? Have they disappointed you? How can too much trust be a form of idolatry?

3. Make a list of famous persons seen on magazine

covers and interviewed often in the media. What have they contributed to the world that makes them worth your attention? Divide these into two lists, one for those who are merely famous, and the second for those worthy of actually following.

4. How does Aung San Suu Kyi belong on the second list? What do you know of Moses that makes him a candidate for this one also?

5. Hymn writer Isaac Watts gazes at the figure of Christ on the cross, where he is impressed by the supreme example of self-giving love. What effect does this have on him, according to the words of his hymn "When I Survey the Wondrous Cross"?

6. Examine your own recent past. What do you find that would commend you as one who would be a good example for the young? Do not let false modesty keep you from recognizing this—nor shame from seeing where you might have set a not-so-worthy example. Without going overboard and emulating Ben Franklin's famous list for self-improvement, what are the areas of your life needing improvement to make you a better example?

HYMN: "When I Survey the Wondrous Cross"

A Prayer

Gracious God, you know our every thought, as well as our deeds, and thus before you there is no hiding. You gave us Jesus the Christ, not only to save us from our bondage to sin and to implant in us the hope of resurrection, but also to serve as an example of how to live. Help us to study him continually in the Gospels and to hold him close to our hearts as we go about our own lives, tempted and also challenged in so many ways. We thank you for the example of others who have followed in his paths, and pray that we too, as we struggle to be the kind of person Christ intends us to be, may yet serve as an example for those who come after us. We lift up and commend to your care Aung San Suu Kyi, who continues to live in danger as she confronts the intractable powers of injustice. Continue to strengthen, guide, and protect her—and all those who dare to speak and act against oppressive powers—that she might stand and eventually triumph in her cause. In Christ's name we pray. Amen.

4. *Broadway Danny Rose* "Acceptance, Forgiveness, Love"

Better is a little with righteousness
than large income with injustice.

Proverbs 16:8

Owe no one anything, except to love one another; for the one who loves another has fulfilled the law. The commandments, "You shall not commit adultery; You shall not murder; You shall not steal; You shall not covet"; and any other commandment, are summed up in this word, "Love your neighbor as yourself." Love does no wrong to a neighbor; therefore, love is the fulfilling of the law.

Romans 13:8–10

"The second is this, 'You shall love your neighbor as yourself.'"

Mark 12:31a

Introduction

Woody Allen's *Broadway Danny Rose* is more upbeat than most of his films. Danny Rose was given his nickname because he was a New York talent agent. Always on the edge of success, he handled acts no one else would touch—a one-armed juggler, a blind xylophone player, a trainer of dancing penguins dressed like rabbis, a tap dancer with a wooden leg, a balloon-folding husband and wife team. Like Christ reaching out to the outcasts, Danny deals with what one character calls "losers." And once Danny helps them achieve success, his legitimately talented acts always leave him for more prestigious agents handling upscale acts—this despite the care that the hapless Danny has lavished on them.

Danny's current act-destined-for-success is a lounge singer named Lou Canova. Danny has dealt with the man's insecurities and frequent lapses into drunkenness with the care of a mother hen. He has taught him little stage tricks, arranged the order of his songs, and, as we enter the picture, is now in the distasteful role of trying to convince Lou's mistress to come and see Lou at the club where Danny has arranged for Milton Berle to catch his act. Danny is not thrilled to learn that Lou has a mistress, but as Lou will not take his advice, he reluctantly has agreed to go visit her. It is not an easy task, because Tina is mad at Lou due to a misunderstanding. Danny follows her around like a bloodhound that refuses to give up the scent, winding up at a mobster's lavish party in New Jersey. The widow of a mobster herself, Tina half listens to her pursuer, then finally calms down enough to agree to go with him as if she were Danny's date to watch Lou perform.

But the mobsters think Danny is romantically involved with Tina. One of them has been courting her, so they give chase to the pair. Tina spots the mobsters at a diner where she and he have discovered that they have opposing views of life and ethics. They flee the restaurant and make their way through the marsh reeds and across the river by tugboat, arriving at Danny's Manhattan apartment where he picks up a few things to hide out in a hotel until Tina can cool the passions of the mobsters.

The Scene

Time into film: 0:48:02   Stop at 0:52:30

Tina is as unimpressed with Danny's seedy lodgings as she had been earlier with Danny's list of the acts he was handling. Her verdict is that he is a loser handling losers. He shows her his pictures of gatherings of performers, but he is always far in the background, or he would be in the picture if the camera range had gone a few feet to one side. Tina's creativity, aroused by her survey of what she calls his "joint," leads her to suggest ways of lightening it up. Although Danny rejects her first idea, he agrees with her tropical motif suggestion. "You do?" she asks in surprise, telling him that nobody before had liked her African jungle arrangement. Encouraged by his assurance that it is great, she reveals that she had dreamt of decorating as a career. Danny tells her that she lacks confidence, that he could see her decorating not just little suburban homes, but hotels and embassies.

Tina is pleased to find someone who believes in her dream, but she demurs, saying it is too late for her, and that her work is ugly. Danny sees her prob-

lem and quotes his Uncle Morris, "the famous dia-
betic from Brooklyn": "If you hate yourself, then you
hate your work." She assures him that she sleeps at
night, that it is Danny who has an ulcer. Danny
explains that his ulcer may be a good thing and
reminds her that although you need laughs, you need
a little suffering also, lest you miss the point of life.
(Earlier Danny had made a similar observation about
the importance of guilt, that we need it lest "we do
terrible things.") Tina rejects this, saying that her
philosophy of life is that it's over quick, so we better
have a good time—"Go for what you want and don't
pay any attention to anyone else. Do it to the other
guy first, because if you don't, he'll do it to you."
Danny, replying that "this sounds more like the
screenplay to *Murder Incorporated*," says that it's no
wonder she doesn't like herself. She is taken aback by
his repetition of the charge and lashes out that he is
the one living like a loser. Danny says that the beauty
of his business is that overnight you can go from "a
bum to a hero" and that is what will happen tonight
with Lou.

Tina quickly interjects that they had better get
going. (She obviously does not want him to dwell on
tonight, because she had arranged for another, more
prestigious agent to show up and steal Lou away from
Danny. She had set this scheme into motion before she
had met and started to like Danny.) As they are about
to leave, Danny gives Tina his ultimate philosophy of
life, again passed on to him by one of his uncles:
"Acceptance, forgiveness, and love." She barely
acknowledges this, so Danny repeats it, telling her as
they leave that he wants to hear more about her decorating idea.

Reflection on the Scene

Although Broadway Danny Rose may be a loser in
some eyes (even at film discussion groups, I find that
many of the men agree with Tina's assessment of him),
his philosophy leads him to focus on what is important
in life—people. And it gifts him with insight into the
human heart. He has known Tina for just a few hours,
but he deduces that she is not comfortable with herself,
that she does not really like the hard-edged, selfish per-
sona she has adopted. No one would have guessed that
beneath her tough exterior dwelt the shriveled soul of
an artist (albeit one that needed a lot of education in
taste!). Danny knows what Jesus knew when he held up
"Love thy neighbor as thyself" as one of the two great
commandments: in order to love your neighbor, you
need to love yourself also.

"Acceptance, forgiveness, and love." Danny's heritage from his Uncle Sidney is a precious one, one that
has shaped his own soul and his relationship with others. Danny is, in Martin Luther's words, "a little
Christ" who reaches out to the lowly and despised. He
works hard shaping their acts so that his clients are the
best they can be; and then he pleads with club owners
and managers to hire them. We see in detail how
Danny has helped Lou come back from his alcohol-
related obscurity to the point where the famous
Milton Berle is about to hire him for his television
special. And we see how Danny's acceptance of Tina
brings out her better nature. She will resist him, following through on her plan of betrayal, but his philosophy will continue to work on her conscience,
finally bringing her around to seek his forgiveness.
That will be the moment of Danny's testing. His heart
has been deeply injured by the betrayal of Lou, when,

accompanied by Tina, he walks out on him on the very night of the success so carefully arranged by Danny. The supreme test for Danny will be the moment when a repentant Tina comes knocking at his door and asks for his "acceptance, forgiveness, and love."

This, of course, is a test we all undergo in our relationships with others. Most people follow Tina's philosophy of grab-what-you-can while you can because life is indeed short. We hear much about a "dog eat dog" world, "it's a jungle out there," "business is business," and "the bottom line." But we know there is a better way, especially those of us who call ourselves Christian. We see in the Gospels the Galilean carpenter daring to live to its fullest the law of love, and we long to do this also. Taught too often to discount ourselves and others, we lapse into the role of sophisticate or cynic, fearing that others will regard us as naive or incompetent if we act toward others in ways of "acceptance, forgiveness, and love." Then, at some point in our lives, when we are faced with the destructiveness of Tina's "do in the other guy first" way, we tentatively try the other way, and are often surprised at the results—the way some respond so positively to us. And even when they reject us, there remains a trace of feeling good that we tried, that we did the right thing regardless of the consequences.

For Further Reflection

1. Have you known someone like Danny—not big or important, perhaps underestimated by others, yet exuding good will and support of neighbors? What effect have they had on others? Yourself? How does the proverb apply to Danny?

2. Who have you known like Tina? What effect on others did they have? Did people turn to them for comfort or support during tough times? How many of the elderly who complain that no one visits them might have been like that—perhaps their own worst enemy in that their grasping personality drives family and friends away?

3. Danny quotes two of his uncles: from where or from whom have you received your basic outlook on life? A family member? Pastor, priest, or church school teacher? How much does the media, especially television and its ads, influence you?

4. How is Danny's philosophy of "acceptance, forgiveness, and love" like the two great commandments Jesus quotes in the twelfth chapter of Mark? Think of a person whom you dislike or from whom you are estranged. How can you show him or her "acceptance, forgiveness, and love"? First, of course, you can pray about and for them, and ask the Spirit to change your own attitude. Then what? A note, a luncheon appointment to share your desire to change things? Rendering help at the office or wherever you encounter the person?

A Prayer

Gracious God, you accept us, forgive us, and love us. Down through the centuries you dealt patiently with your people Israel as you tried to fashion them into a servant people. Through laws and prophets you commanded and pleaded with them to adopt your gracious ways. Then you sent your Son to be the Suffering Servant for the whole world, making it possible for our Gentile ancestors also to be included with your people. Christ reached out to the rejects of his society, including them in your circle of love. We know this, yet daily we disappoint you, and daily we pray that you will "forgive us our sins, as we forgive those who sin against us"—and daily you do so. Help us to continue to walk firmly and gently in your Son's way of acceptance, forgiveness, and love. By your spirit strengthen our resolve to widen our circle of acceptance, that others also will be drawn to you. We ask this in Christ's name. Amen.

5. *Chocolat*
How to Measure Goodness

> When an alien resides with you in your land, you shall not oppress the alien. The alien who resides with you shall be to you as the citizen among you; you shall love the alien as yourself, for you were aliens in the land of Egypt: I am the LORD your God.
>
> Leviticus 19:33–34

> The LORD is a stronghold for the oppressed,
>   a stronghold in times of trouble.
> And those who know your name put their trust in
>   you,
>   for you, O LORD, have not forsaken those who
>   seek you.
>
> Psalm 9:9–10

> When he came to Nazareth, where he had been brought up, he went to the synagogue on the sabbath day, as was his custom. He stood up to read, and the scroll of the prophet Isaiah was given to him. He unrolled the scroll and found the place where it was written:

"The Spirit of the Lord is upon me,
    because he has anointed me
    to bring good news to the poor.
He has sent me to proclaim release to the captives
    and recovery of sight to the blind,
    to let the oppressed go free,
to proclaim the year of the Lord's favor."

And he rolled up the scroll, gave it back to the attendant, and sat down. The eyes of all in the synagogue were fixed on him. Then he began to say to them, "Today this scripture has been fulfilled in your hearing."

Luke 4:16–21

Introduction

Lasse Hallstrom's *Chocolat* is a delightful tale with a touch of fantasy and whimsy laced throughout, like tasty peanuts in a chocolate treat. Though probably too sophisticated and a bit too long for young children, the film's themes of hospitality and tolerance make it suitable for a wide variety of cocoa lovers, young and old. Even coffee addicts should be able to enjoy the sumptuous scenes in which rich, creamy chocolate is made into all sorts of tempting confections. Set in the picturesque French village of Lansquenet, where "nothing has changed in over a hundred years," the story depicts the wrenching changes faced by individuals and the community when the North Wind blows Vianne Rocher and her daughter Anouk into town. Theirs has been a nomadic life, with mother and daughter constantly on the move due to circumstances that are not revealed to us but that we can guess, based on what we see in this story.

Vianne is a master chocolatier, so she rents a vacant shop from the town's seventy-year-old libertine Armande Voizin and, with her daughter, begins to scrub and clean it. Their view of the interior blocked by wrapping paper taped over the store windows, the villagers speculate what their mysterious new resident is up to. The local nobleman and mayor of the town, Comte De Reynaud, is not so reticent as they. He boldly enters her shop to welcome her and to invite her to mass. Vianne thanks him but turns down his invitation. Visibly perturbed, De Reynaud is even more upset to learn that she is planning to open a chocolaterie, even though the Lenten season is upon them. The count believes that the opening of a shop selling something so frivolous is very inappropriate, this being a time when the faithful give up luxuries. Soon he is spreading his view around town, turning the villagers against what he regards as an atheistic interloper.

Some in the town, however, welcome Vianne and her magical chocolate. She has a mysterious way of determining just the right kind of chocolate for each person, the delicious brew or bon bon bringing a sense of relief and freedom to the consumer. The bitter and cynical Armande, whose own daughter has kept her boy away from his grandmother because of what she perceives as her wicked ways, mellows after drinking Vianne's cocoa. She soon becomes a staunch defender of the town's newest resident. Vianne's magical chocolate brings relief to many others as well: a faded marriage is rejuvenated; an abused wife finds the courage to stand up to and leave her brutish husband; and a river gypsy is welcomed when the suspicious townsfolk reject him and his people. Nor does change stop with these folk. Vianne, finding herself at the head of a small, caring fellowship, changes for the better (especially in the eyes of her daughter). Just when she is on the verge of giving up and leaving town because of the Comte De Reynaud's campaign against her, her friends rally around.

Comte De Reynaud's chief weapon against Vianne has been the church. The young, new pastor is inexperienced and willing to let the most powerful man in town lead him into denouncing the chocolate shop and its proprietor. The count even previews and rewrites the hapless clergyman's sermons. Another ally of the count is Caroline, Armande's very proper daughter, who is fearful that the combination of chocolate shop and her mother will corrupt her son. But at long last, after a series of near tragic and comic events, even the count and Caroline undergo a transformation. Like any story billed as a comedy, "all's well that ends well." Our scenes are almost the last ones in the film.

The Scene

Time into film: 1:50:32   Stop at 1:53:45

It is Easter Sunday, and the priest Pere Henri ascends the high pulpit to deliver his homily. The church is filled with villagers, including the count, who has just gone through a humiliating experience that leaves him open to new possibilities. Pere Henri begins somewhat awkwardly by saying that he does not know what he wants to preach about this Sunday—but he knows it is not about the divine transformation that brought Christ back from the dead. "I'd rather talk about his humanity," he says, "I mean, you know, how he lived his life on earth. His kindness, his tolerance." He urges them to listen, stating, for perhaps the first time in this pulpit, what he himself thinks: "We can't go around measuring our goodness by what we don't do, by what we resist, and who we exclude." The camera roves through the crowded sanctuary, showing us close-ups of the people who need to hear the priest's message. "I think we have to measure goodness by what we embrace, by what we create, and whom we include," he tells them.

The narrator remarks that this sermon was not the most eloquent or fiery that Pere Henri would preach, but that it brought a new sensation that day, a "lightening of the spirit." This is evident in the faces of the major characters that we see. Even the count seems to agree, something confirmed a few moments later.

As the churchgoers emerge from their church, the celebration of spring that Vianne had been planning is taking place. Jugglers, acrobats, and food venders vie for the crowd's attention. Vianne is there passing out samples of her deliciously potent chocolates. There is much merriment and singing. Pere Henri is thoroughly enjoying the proceedings. So is the count. He looks across the square, and, catching the attention of Vianne, offers a friendly nod of approval. She returns the gesture with her winning smile.

Reflection on the Scene

If the church where she had lived had practiced what the young priest finally espouses, Vianne probably would not have left it. Whether or not she will return to its worship, she has long shown that she embraces the teachings of its Founder. She has brought "good news to the poor" and proclaimed "release to the captives and recovery of sight to the blind." Whether conscious of it or not, her party in the square is a celebration of the One who lets "the oppressed go free." The people of the village, including their spiritual leader, had forgotten God's commandment to "love the alien as yourself" when they boycotted Vianne's store because she welcomed into her shop the despised riverboat people. When she gave shelter to the wife fleeing from her abusive husband, the count and the villagers regarded her as breaking up a home and undermining the authority of husbands, but she was following in the steps of the psalmist who saw the Lord as "the stronghold for the oppressed."

Vianne's struggle for justice was difficult, but the celebration and reconciliation show that it was worth the effort. Our own struggles might not be as dramatic, nor our victories as clear-cut as in the movie, but we too will be able to join in a victory celebration. As the author of Psalm 9 declares a little later (v. 18), "For the needy shall not always be forgotten, nor the hope of the poor perish forever." During the many costly struggles of the last half of the twentieth century, few of us could have predicted such a relatively bloodless dismantling of the Berlin Wall or of apartheid in South Africa. No one who saw the jubilant crowds dancing on and before the Wall, or the seemingly mile-long lines of blacks waiting patiently in line to vote for the first time, will ever be able to forget those images of joy. We too can appreciate the little victories over wrong in our offices, churches, or neighborhoods—if we persevere in what we believe is right.

For Further Reflection

1. What wrongs need to be righted at your work-place, school, or community? Are they recognized as problems, or are they ignored? Who says that things are just as they are and cannot be changed?

2. What risks have you, like Vianne, taken to change

the status quo? Whom have you known who has stayed outside the church, yet still followed in the footsteps of the prophets and of Christ in seeking justice and reconciliation?

3. Try this simple experiment at the next coffee hour at your church: stand to one side and see if most people gather with those they already know. Who is standing around alone? Do they stay very long? (These questions arise out of the author's frequent experiences of guest teaching at a number of large churches and never being approached by someone not in the class. It seems that the more the pastor declares during announcements how "friendly our church is," the more lonely seems to be the fellowship hour experience for a stranger.) What can you do to insure that this does not happen at your church?

HYMN: "Called as Partners in Christ's Service"

A Prayer

O God, who is like the shepherd going out to seek the lost sheep, we thank you that in our baptism you have welcomed us into your fold. May we be imitators of your Christ so that there will never be a person unwelcomed in our church or community; never a cause for justice without an advocate; never a silence of oppression not broken by a word or song of encouragement. We thank you for those who answer your call to serve, inside and outside the church, and we pray that you will give us the courage to be among them. In the name of the One who welcomed all, we pray. Amen.

6. *A Civil Action*
The True Worth of a Life

O LORD, you God of vengeance,
  you God of vengeance, shine forth!
Rise up, O judge of the earth;
  give to the proud what they deserve!
O LORD, how long shall the wicked,
  how long shall the wicked exult?
They pour out their arrogant words;
  all the evildoers boast.
They crush your people, O LORD,
  and afflict your heritage.
They kill the widow and the stranger,
  they murder the orphan,
and they say, "The LORD does not see;
  the God of Jacob does not perceive."

. . . .

Who rises up for me against the wicked?
  Who stands up for me against evildoers?

Psalm 94:1–7, 16

"Take care! Be on your guard against all kinds of
greed; for one's life does not consist in the abundance of possessions."

Luke 12:15

Of course, there is great gain in godliness combined with contentment; for we brought nothing
into the world, so that we can take nothing out of
it; but if we have food and clothing, we will be
content with these. But those who want to be
rich fall into temptation and are trapped by many
senseless and harmful desires that plunge people
into ruin and destruction. For the love of money
is a root of all kinds of evil, and in their eagerness

to be rich some have wandered away from the
faith and pierced themselves with many pains.

1 Timothy 6:6–10

Introduction

A Civil Action tells of the transformation of lawyer Jan
Schlichtmann in this true-life story adapted from the
book by Jonathan Harr. Schlichtmann and his partners
are on a fast track to wealth and glory, handling personal injury suits that pay big rewards. Jan carefully
chooses cases that are so clear-cut that a company will
settle out of court rather than face a long and costly lit-
igation process. He enjoys wearing tailored suits, driving a fancy car, and living in a house that advertises his
wealth and status. When a partner brings in a new
wrongful death case, Jan nixes it at first—the plaintiffs
are blue collar, so the rewards do not seem lucrative
enough. But when Jan visits the home of Anne
Anderson, whose child died from leukemia, something
about her and the story of the death touches him. He
agrees to take the case. The other parents of the neighborhood who lost their children to leukemia are all
convinced that it was contaminated water dumped by
two corporations that was the cause of their children's
illness. But the corporations denied any blame, and the
parents lacked resources to prove otherwise.

Jan takes the case, confident that he can win, even
though his opponents are two of the largest corporations in the country—W.R. Grace and Co. and
Beatrice Foods. It will be a David vs. Goliath story;
everyone knows that little David won that battle. But
not this time. A battery of big-city lawyers, chief of
whom is Jerome Facher, senior partner in one of
Boston's most prestigious firms, represents "Goliath."

Their pockets are deep, and their knowledge of the labyrinthine ways of delaying and using the law is great. The costs of testing the neighborhood's soil and water and tracking down the identity of those disposing of wastes, a staggering $2.6 million, has to be covered by Jan and his partners. Their fear rises, but Jan's confidence in his ability to win is unwavering. He refuses to heed his partners' advice, and when he turns down an offer to settle, their fear rises to near panic level. Although there is a positive postscript, *A Civil Action* ends very differently from the usual lawyer-as-hero film—in a bankruptcy court. Jan has to part with his house, his car, and virtually all of his assets.

The Scene

Time into film: 1:47:17   Stop at black screen

Jan is sitting at a table, and as the woman judge speaks, we learn that this is a bankruptcy hearing: "The purpose of these questions is not to embarrass or humiliate, but rather to verify the information you have declared as your assets." "I understand," he quietly replies, obviously somewhat embarrassed by the proceedings.

"Because," the judge continues, "what you're asking your creditors to believe with this petition is—well, it's hard to believe—" "I know," he interjects. "—that after seventeen years of practicing law, all you have to show for it is $14 in a checking account and a portable radio?"

"That's correct," he replies. She shakes her head, and asks, "Where did it go? The money, the property, the personal belongings—things by which one measure's one's life?" He looks at her, smiles slightly, and shakes his head. "What happened?" she inquires. Jan looks down, the man once full of cleverly phrased arguments now at a loss for words. The screen fades to black.

Reflection on the Scene

Unlike the judge, we have witnessed Jan's story and can appreciate the irony of her words. Like the fictional Broadway Danny Rose, Jan Schlichtmann might look like a loser to the movers and shakers of society, but in the world that matters most, he has gained a great victory. He has learned the hard way what Jesus taught: "Be on your guard against all kinds of greed; for one's life does not consist in the abundance of possessions." The judge follows the script of the world and regards Jan as one of life's losers because he possesses none of the things by which the world values a person. Jan, truly taking the side of the little people oppressed by the corporations and spending his all in defending their case, has been led to follow a far different script, one that leads him back to his soul.

In a society in which almost every public message agrees with the judge's assessment about the value of a person's life, this movie is very important. In the epilogue we are told that Jan was able to pay off his debts after several years. He took up again the practice of law. But it was not the same, self-aggrandizing law practice as before. He continues to come to the aid of both the little people, up against the "principalities and powers" of the corporate world, and the environment, so little valued by most corporations.

Reflecting on the life of Jan Schlichtmann, we might think about what our own life adds up to. How do others regard us? More important, of course, how do we measure our worth? More important even than this, what do we think Christ might say about our life's work?

For Further Reflection

1. How do you feel when someone states, "The person with the most toys at the end wins"? What might you say in response?

2. What do television ads say is important in life? Why are they so persuasive? Check out the statistics on the amount spent on luxuries or beverages and cigarettes and compare the totals with what is given to churches and charities.

3. Make two lists: one of your assets, the things and money you own; the other of the people you know and good experiences you have had. Which could you most easily give up? Note that one ad campaign seems to realize that there is something more to life than possessing things: it shows some tender moments we spend with loved ones and friends, with the narrator saying that some things cannot be bought, but for the rest there is a credit card.

4. This would be a good scene to share with people during the church's annual stewardship campaign. How is Jan's new lifestyle an example of good stewardship? Why does the church say that talent and time are as important as money in stewardship?

5. Parents and grandparents should read the classic Dr. Seuss story "How the Grinch Stole Christmas" and discuss with their children that climactic line, "Maybe Christmas isn't something that comes from a store, maybe Christmas is something more." (But do

not use the over-blown feature film that negates the message! Use the book or the wonderful half-hour video originally shown on television.)

HYMN: "God of Grace and God of Glory" (Especially note the third stanza and the plea "Shame our wanton selfish gladness / Rich in things and poor in soul.")

A Prayer

O God, who is the source of all that we have and are, we confess that at times we have been like the lawyer in our film, "rich in things and poor in soul." We thank you that you have placed within us a yearning that no amount of things can satisfy. By your Spirit help us to treasure those things that bind us to one another: faith, hope and love. Help us to possess our things, rather than allowing them to possess us. In a world so full of tempting goods, help us to withstand their allure so that we might use them for the benefit of others, and not just of ourselves. In the name of the One who had no place to lay his head we pray. Amen.

7. *The Color Purple*
The Return of the Prodigal Daughter

Create in me a clean heart, O God,
    and put a new and right spirit within me.
Do not cast me away from your presence,
    and do not take your holy spirit from me.
Restore to me the joy of your salvation,
    and sustain in me a willing spirit.

Psalm 51:10–12

"Just so, I tell you, there is joy in the presence
of the angels of God over one sinner who
repents. . . .
"Then the son said to him, 'Father, I have sinned
against heaven and before you; I am no longer
worthy to be called your son.'"

Luke 15:10, 21

From now on, therefore, we regard no one from
a human point of view; even though we once
knew Christ from a human point of view, we
know him no longer in that way. So if anyone is
in Christ, there is a new creation: everything old
has passed away; see, everything has become
new! All this is from God, who reconciled us to
himself through Christ, and has given us the
ministry of reconciliation; that is, in Christ God
was reconciling the world to himself, not counting their trespasses against them, and entrusting
the message of reconciliation to us.

2 Corinthians 5:16–19

Introduction

Director Steven Spielberg is well known for adding a
note of optimism or lightness to a dark source, as in
his adaptation of James Ballard's dark-toned novel
Empire of the Sun, about a boy in a Japanese internment camp. His approach to Alice Walker's novel *The
Color Purple* is an even better case in point. He invents
a scene not found in the novel, the reuniting of juke-
joint singer Shug Avery with her preacher father.
Although the relationship of Shug with her father is a
subplot in both novel and film, Spielberg's addition
provides an emotional high in the film, a parallel to

Celie's unexpected, triumphant return to her mother's homestead and the eventual reunion with her stolen children.

The novel and film, of course, center on Celie, the perpetual victim of sexual abuse by the man she had regarded as her father, and then by her husband. While still almost a child herself (despite having given birth to two babies, which her ruthless "father" wrested from her and gave away), she is sold to a seemingly charming man she knows only as "Mister." Once in her new home, Mister turns out to be a brutal master who sees Celie merely as a sex object and housekeeper. He even has the gall to bring home his sick mistress, Shug Avery, so that Celie can nurse her back to health. He had not counted on the two women becoming friends, Shug seeing beauty in the neglected woman whom he regarded as ugly. Shug restores a sense of dignity and hope to Celie, eventually even becoming the means for her to reconnect with the sister that Mister had parted her from many years earlier.

As much as Shug Avery helps Celie, the strong-willed woman finds that she cannot help herself. For many years she has been estranged from her father, who pastors a nearby church. Apparently they had parted ways when she gave up singing in church for the more lucrative singing in juke joints. We see her twice in the film attempt to reconcile with Reverend Avery: once when he drives by in his buggy, and another time when she goes to his church to tell him she is going away. Both times he turns away from her without a word. But near the end of the film, when Shug has returned from the city to renew Celie's courage and help set her free, she tries again for reconciliation.

The Scene

Time into film: 2:18:02   Stop at 2:24:56

A crowd moves toward Harpo's Juke Joint, where Shug is holding forth in the lively song that years before had so raised the spirit of Celie, "Miss Celie's Blues." The camera cuts to Rev. Avery's church, where a service is in progress. The worshipers can hear the music from the juke joint. A woman says to the minister, who is ignoring the song and still preaching, "Shhhh, Reverend. God's trying to tell you something!" Someone from the choir joins in, "Yes, God's trying to tell you something." The choir rises and breaks out in song. Back at the juke joint Shug begins to sing, "Speak, Lord," the jazzy music beginning to blend with the church gospel music.

Led by Shug, the juke-joint patrons leave the building and begin to cross the little bridge connecting the nightspot with the river shore. Clearly, Shug is heading for the church. As she, the band, and the patrons head down the lane, they continue to sing, "Speak, Lord, I love you, Lord." At the church the choir is also singing, adding to "Speak, Lord" the words directed at the minister, "Maybe God's trying to tell you something!" Arriving at the church, Shug opens the door and comes in. The band and singing sinners follow right behind. The worshipers are surprised, but none as much as Shug's father. He is speechless, a rare state for a man of the pulpit. He takes off his glasses in disbelief. All the while almost everyone is singing the high-energy song "Speak, Lord, God is trying to tell you something right now."

Shug marches down the aisle, as do her followers. The church members are on their feet too. Marching right up to the pulpit, daughter embraces father. This time he does not turn away. Shug whispers to him, "See, Daddy, sinners have souls, too." We see tears in Celie's eyes, as well as in those of father and daughter.

The music continues at its energetic level as it wafts over to the farm where Mister still lives. At the mailbox a hand pulls out a registered letter on which is stamped "Immigration and Naturalization Service." We surmise that it is about Celie's children, whom she has learned are in Africa. We see a chicken coop and a hand opening a metal box. There is a lot of money in the box. Mister takes it out. In town we see him enter the courthouse. He stands before a door, on the glass window of which are the words "Immigration and Naturalization Service." He goes inside, where we see him talking at length with a man at the desk. The joyful music fades out as the screen darkens.

Reflection on the Scene

Although some literary purists criticized Mr. Spielberg for this scene, most of us loved it. Even novelist Alice Walker is said to have approved of Mr. Spielberg's addition. Like the climax of the great parable told by Jesus about the Father and Two Sons, the scene shows the joy of reconciliation. It adds to the power of Celie's own triumph over adversity. Shug Avery's long period of painful separation from her father is over. The sinner has come home, and the hard heart of the righteous has melted (even though a minister, her father had been more like the elder brother than the compassionate father of Jesus' parable). Surely the angels in heaven are singing with joy.

As Frederick Buechner says in the title of one of his books, *The Longing For Home*, a yearning to return to the home God provides for us is ingrained deeply within us. The Bible story is based on this longing and on our struggle to accept the terms of God's promise to return us home. Anyone who has experienced estrangement from a loved one, be it parent, spouse, family member, or close friend, knows something of the pain of Shug Avery. There is an empty space in our hearts and souls that nothing else can fill. No amount of money and things, fame or prestige can fill this void. Shug looms big in the eyes of her lover, of Celie, and of the juke-joint customers, but this cannot compensate for the loss of her father's respect and love.

We cannot always go back and find reconciliation with an estranged one. The person might be dead or too far removed by distance or time. But we can discover that deeper reconciliation on which our reconciliation with all others depends. We can repent with the psalmist who pleads with God for "a clean heart." We can accept Paul's assurance that anyone who accepts Christ becomes a new creation. We can place our broken relationships and the persons from whom we are estranged into God's hands in the belief that all that is now broken will one day be made whole in Christ. The amazing thing in the movie is that even the abusive Mister shares in the abundant grace of the moment. We see what Celie and friends do not, that it is Mister's effort with the government agency that makes possible the return not just of Celie's lost children, but of the new families they have formed in Africa as well.

For Further Reflection

1. What family rift(s) have you suffered? As you think back, what was the cause? Was it major or

minor? Have you, like Shug, made attempts at reconciliation? What were the results?

2. How can Shug's reconciliation keep your hope
and efforts alive, even in the face of rejection?

3. If the person is still living, how can the following
become an effective part of a strategy for obtaining
reconciliation: letters, telephone calls, e-mails, a visit,
gifts, other people as mediators, and, of course, prayer?

4. Even if attempts at reconciliation are rejected or
impossible, how can such attempts benefit us? What spiritual "payoff" is there (such as in the case of Mister, who
never rejoins Celie but watches her reunion from afar)?

HYMN: "Amazing Grace"

A Prayer

Gracious God, you show us in Scripture how you made
us to be at home with you in our world, but we have too
often decided to go our own way. We have fallen out with
family and friends because of injuries, real and imagined.
Send into our hearts, minds, and souls your gentle Spirit
of peace and wisdom, calling us away from our desires
and ourselves so that we might discover your way. Help
us to forgive and to seek forgiveness, to reach out rather
than to rebuff, to love rather than to seek revenge. We
thank you for the hope and promise of reconciliation
given by Jesus in his wonderful stories, and even for
reflections of those promises in novels and films. Keep
strong our faith that in Christ you are reconciling the
world to yourself, not counting our trespasses against us.
It is in his name that we pray this. Amen.

8. *Come See the Paradise*
Santa Might Say "No,"
But Christ Always Says "Yes"

And the foreigners who join themselves to the
    LORD,
  to minister to him, to love the name of the
    LORD,
  and to be his servants,
all who keep the sabbath, and do not profane it,
  and hold fast my covenant—
these I will bring to my holy mountain,
  and make them joyful in my house of prayer.
Isaiah 56:6–7a

"Let the little children come to me; do not
stop them; for it is to such as these that the kingdom of God belongs. Truly I tell you, whoever
does not receive the kingdom of God as a little
child will never enter it." And he took them up in
his arms, laid his hands on them, and blessed
them.
Mark 10:14b–16

Introduction

War always brings to the surface hostility and prejudice, not only against our foreign enemy but also
against anyone who looks like them or reminds us of
them. This was especially true during World War II in
those Pacific coast states with a concentration of
Japanese Americans. Alan Parker's *Come See the
Paradise* effectively dramatizes their plight. In the late
1930s Jack McGurn and Lily Kawamura fall in love,
and even though her family is not pleased with the

match, they marry and produce a beautiful daughter. Then comes Pearl Harbor, and the prejudice and envy of the white population is unleashed against their neighbors of Japanese ancestry. The Japanese Americans have not yet been rounded up and herded into concentration camps, but the atmosphere is filled with hostility toward them.

The Scene

Time into film: 1:09:22   Stop at 1:11:20

Shortly after the bombing of Pearl Harbor, Jack is taking his little daughter shopping in a large department store. Like the other proud fathers, he takes her to see the store Santa Claus. They take their place in line and wait for their turn. Jack pays no attention to a dark stare from another parent. It is now their turn, and Jack sets his little daughter on the knee of Santa. The man takes one look at the little girl and refuses to listen to her, calling her a Jap. Jack is incensed that an adult would be so rude and cruel to his daughter. The Santa tells Jack that he isn't going to speak to any Jap kid. The father angrily refuses to go away, until a floor manager and security officer appear on the scene. The little girl is heartbroken, unable to understand why Santa has said no to her. Jack, with daughter in tow, leaves the store.

Reflection on the Scene

Children are often victims of the cruelties of war, even on the homefront if they look too much like the enemy. Just how much Santa Claus is identified with our culture is shown in this sad scene. Not only does he lure families into the store for commercial reasons, he also shares and reinforces the prevailing prejudice of the time. The attempt of Jesus' disciples to keep away the children pales in comparison to the heartless rejection of a little girl by the now secular department store saint. Jesus bid his disciples to call into question any aspect of society that oppressed or dehumanized its members. Here we see a saintly figure affirm and even reinforce the prejudice that is so injurious to a child.

The scene is out of the distant past of World War II, and yet we saw similar incidents following the terrible events of the 9-11 terrorist attacks in 2001. Almost everyone who looked like a Middle Easterner became fearful for their safety, and even their lives. A few were killed by angry persons seeking revenge. One man who killed a Pakistani father of four girls said it was the right thing to do. Thus this film, set in a past sixty years distant, is timely still.

The scene also should remind the church that at times it has been like that store Santa, espousing the values of its culture, even when they are contrary to the gospel. The church is still one of the most segregated institutions of our society, and for many years it preached the separation of races in the South and practiced it in the North as well. Christ deserves better of his followers. May we do all that we can to see that no one is ever excluded because of race or other factors.

For Further Reflection

1. How or where have you seen or heard of a child being excluded? On what basis?

2. What do you teach about Santa Claus? How does the secular carol "Santa Claus is Coming to Town" teach a doctrine of "works righteous"? (That is, that we are of value or acceptable only when we are "good"?

Or, in the case of Jack's daughter, only if she were white.)

3. What groups or leaders in your community are working for the welfare of children? How are children treated in your church? Out of sight, out of mind? What efforts are there to make them feel welcome and included in your services and activities? How can you help in this?

HYMN: "In Christ There Is No East or West"

A Prayer

O God, how your Son loved children, and how they seemed to love him! We know that he declared that those who follow him must become like a child in their hearts, but we too often value sophistication more than simplicity; firmly held convictions rather than open-ness to differences; smug self-control, to joyous aban-donment. Help us to see how precious children are, and how damaging any prejudiced word or act of exclusion is to them—and to ourselves. Knock our socks off when we grow stuffy or complacent by bring-ing us into close contact with children. May we see and love the same things in them that our Lord saw and loved. This we ask in the name of your Son. Amen.

9. *Contact*
Awesome Universe, Awesome God

The heavens are telling the glory of God;
    and the firmament proclaims his handiwork.
Day to day pours forth speech,
    and night to night declares knowledge.

There is no speech, nor are there words;
  their voice is not heard;
yet their voice goes out through all the earth,
  and their words to the end of the world.

Psalm 19:1–4

O LORD, our Sovereign,
  how majestic is your name in all the earth!

You have set your glory above the heavens.
  Out of the mouths of babes and infants
you have founded a bulwark because of your foes,
  to silence the enemy and the avenger.

When I look at your heavens, the work of your
    fingers,
  the moon and the stars that you have estab-
    lished;
what are human beings that you are mindful of
    them,
  mortals that you care for them?

You have made them a little lower than God,
  and crowned them with glory and honor.

Psalm 8:1–5

In the beginning was the Word . . .

John 1:1a

He is the image of the invisible God, the first-
born of all creation; for in him all things in
heaven and on earth were created, things visible
and invisible, whether thrones or dominions or
rulers or powers—all things have been created
through him and for him.

Colossians 1:15–16

Introduction

Contact, director Robert Zemeckis' film, based on Carl Sagan's novel, explores the relationship between science and faith. Ever since Copernicus and Galileo observed that the earth is not the center of the solar system, there has been what some call a war between science and religion. This more properly should be called a war between science and the church, because it is the church that saw its traditional teachings about the physical universe threatened by the new learning, and therefore acted to silence those who called those teachings into question. The first scientists were themselves believers who wanted to correct some aspects of the church's worldview, not destroy the faith. This warfare grew far more intense in the nineteenth and early twentieth centuries with the publication of the writings of Charles Darwin and Sigmund Freud, each one in his own way calling into question church doctrines based on a literal reading of the Scriptures.

Many theologians were able to accommodate the new findings by breaking away from the literal interpretation of the Bible. The first of these church leaders often were attacked by their peers, with some of the pioneers losing their pulpits or teaching positions. But gradually these thinkers' ideas prevailed in many denominations. At the same time, the church was losing its stranglehold on the larger culture as the result of the sciences flooding society with a deluge of new marvels—steam power, the cotton gin and spinning machines, the electric light, the internal combustion engine, the airplane, and much more. But still the old war continues, with many believers advocating that creationism, based on a literal interpretation of the Bible, be taught in schools on the same level as evolution.

It is against this background that the story of Ellie Arroway is told. Raised by a father who taught her to think and always to ask questions, she became obsessed as a young girl with making contact with the life forms that she believes must exist out there in the universe. She gives up any faith she might have had in God when her father is struck down by a heart attack and unable to reach his heart pills. She grows into a young woman who follows her dream into her chosen profession, that of a radio astronomer searching the heavens for some contact with another species. When it comes, she embarks on a hazardous journey, not just into the depths of space, but also into the depths of the human spirit or soul. It becomes a quest in which she learns that faith and science need not be enemies but fellow companions for those embarked on the journey called Life.

The Scene

Time into film: 0:00:00   Stop at 0:03:51

Our scene begins right after the movie title *Contact* fades to black, and it continues for just a few seconds short of four minutes. After a brief moment of darkness and silence, there is the jarring noise of rock music and voices, as we see from outer space the southeastern portion of the United States still in the darkness of night. The outline of the curved horizon is aglow, and within a moment we see the sun, and the pencil-thin outline of light grows wider, until the earth, from which we are receding, looks like a beautiful crescent moon. The songs and voices are changing rapidly, creating a Babel-like effect. We quickly pass the Moon, and then the red planet Mars seems to glide by. We hear snatches of voices—some of them astronauts—

and music, as we pass through the asteroid belt. The huge orb of Jupiter, ringed by several of its moons, speeds by. We hear voices from the civil rights and the Vietnam war era—Martin Luther King Jr. and John F. Kennedy.

Then we are speeding through Saturn's rings, and we behold its ringed beauty in its entirety. All the while the disk of the sun is growing smaller and smaller. By now the voices are from the 1940s, then the '50s—the Lone Ranger, Franklin Delano Roosevelt, and Adolf Hitler. As we pass out of our solar system, the sound turns to static, and then ceases altogether. We pass by a double star, probably Alpha Centaurus, our nearest star neighbor. In silence we pass through several nebulae, some of them glowing. Traveling at an impossible speed, far beyond the barrier of the speed of light (186,000 miles per second), we emerge from our own galaxy, soon able to see its glowing, globular center, and its pinwheel-like arms, consisting of billions of stars. The journey continues in silence, passing by star clusters, spiral galaxies, and glowing nebulae. Now we are speeding to the very limits of the universe so that what seemed to be separate lights are now forming a long series of streaks lighting up the screen.

There is a blaze of white light, and then the scene turns into what looks like a reflection, the reflection of a window. It is the reflection from a bedroom window in the retina of a human eye, an eye magnified so as to seemingly encompass the universe. The camera pulls back, revealing that the eye belongs to a young girl. We are now in the bedroom of Ellie Arroway, who is operating a ham radio. She is making contact with someone far away, thus giving us a foretaste of the story that is to come.

Reflection on the Scene

The almost-four-minute scene is a tour de force of special effects and camera work. We are given what amounts to a brief tour of the universe, as we know it, and then returned to the small eye of the beholder. The spectacle we are treated to arouses awe and wonder. When the camera takes us into the eye of the girl, the words of Psalm 8 are appropriate: "O LORD, our Lord, how majestic is thy name in all the earth."

I recently showed the scene to a group and asked how they felt afterward. A woman replied, "Small." Another said, "Awe." Someone added, "Insignificant." And so we might feel, our earth and sun being such a tiny part of the universe, as the scene shows so well. This is how the psalmist must have felt, gazing upward with the unaided eye and seeing how great the number of stars are, for as he looked at the heavenly objects made by God, he was led to ask about the nature and significance of human beings—who are we, so tiny in comparison to the heavenly objects, that God should care for us? His answer obviously derived from the collection of stories about God and the covenant people that was his heritage. Forming the Hebrew Scriptures, these stories affirmed that we are made in the image of God, and thus "a little lower than God." Into our hands God has entrusted the earth and its creatures, so that the psalmist ends his psalm of awe and wonder as he began it, with a note of praise, "O LORD, our Lord, how majestic is thy name in all the earth!"

Some fearful believers feel that the discoveries of astronomy, revealing a universe vaster than the human mind can even comprehend, diminish our view of God. In actuality, the discoveries of science can enlarge our view of our Creator. Hymn writer Henry Hallam Tweedy must have thought so when he wrote, "Eternal God, whose power upholds both flower and flaming star / To whom there is no here nor there, no time, no near nor far / No alien race, no foreign shore, no child unsought, unknown: / O send us forth, thy prophets true, to make all lands thine own!" Many years ago the British scholar J. B. Phillips wrote a book that I wish Ellie in our story could read—*Your God is Too Small.* Our problem is not that science and faith conflict, but that our understanding of both our faith and the universe sometimes conflict. And when they do, we need to reexamine that understanding. The poet Tennyson put it well in his hymn-poem "Strong Son of God, Immortal Love": "Our little systems have their day; they have their day and cease to be; / They are but broken lights of Thee, And Thou, O Lord, art more than they." Writing at a time when the new sciences seemed to be eating away like acid at the church's faith, Tennyson could see that it was jealously guarded theological systems that were threatened, not the faith itself.

We grow in our faith when new facts and theories confront us. Led by the Spirit, the source of all truth and creativity, we can with confidence sift the untrue from the core of our faith, free of any fear that our faith will crumble. Ellie has to learn that even her science is based on a type of faith, one that cannot be proven in a laboratory. If we could "prove" such a God, it would not be the God of Scriptures, but a god far too small for the mysteries and wonders that lie ahead.

For Further Reflection

1. Spend a few minutes outside gazing at the stars. Bring a pair of binoculars or a telescope mounted on a tripod. Note how many more stars can be seen with such aids, and how many seemingly single stars are doubles. Read again Psalm 8.

2. Have you experienced any faith "growing pains" or crises due to what you have learned in science courses and what you are taught at church? Or has your church and its leaders been able to work out a relationship between the two disciplines?

3. How does it help to believe that science is the way we approach the physical world but that it cannot answer questions of "why?" or "what does it mean?"—and that faith is the way we deal with the whys and questions of meaning?

HYMN: "Eternal God, Whose Power Upholds" or "The Spacious Firmament on High"

A Prayer

This time use the words of the third stanza of Henry Hallam Tweedy's hymn "Eternal God, Whose Power Upholds."

O God of truth, whom science seeks, and reverent
    souls adore,
Who lightest every earnest mind, of every clime
    and shore,
Dispel the gloom of error's night, of ignorance and
    fear,
Until true wisdom from above shall make life's
    pathway clear!
Amen.

10. *Dancing at Lughnasa*
A Moment of Abandonment to Joy

David danced before the LORD with all his
might. . . .

2 Samuel 6:14a

Praise the LORD!
Sing to the LORD a new song,
   his praise in the assembly of the faithful.
Let Israel be glad in its Maker;
   let the children of Zion rejoice in their King.
Let them praise his name with dancing,
   making melody to him with tambourine and
      lyre.
For the LORD takes pleasure in his people;
   he adorns the humble with victory.

Psalm 149:1-4

"Very truly, I tell you, you will weep and mourn,
but the world will rejoice; you will have pain, but
your pain will turn into joy."

John 16:20

Introduction

Life has not been kind to the five Mundy sisters. It is
1936 in Ireland, a troubled land from which many of
the men have fled seeking freedom or work. In this
fiercely religious land more men enter the priesthood
than women become nuns, so the ratio of eligible men
to single women is heavily weighted against the sisters,
especially in the countryside far from a city. Only one
of the sisters, the imperious Kate, has obtained enough
education to be able to find an outside job, teaching in
the local church school. Maggie tends the hearth, her

big-heartedness managing to mitigate the law-obsessed dictates of prim and proper Kate. Agnes is sweet and eccentric, her serenity helping to keep the family on an even keel. Simple-minded Rose will never be able to fend for herself, but her innocence and vulnerability evokes compassion from her sisters. Christina is the lonely romantic who eight years before gave way to the passion elicited by her lover Gerry. Young Michael was the result, a curious, creative child surrounded by the love of his aunts as well as his mother. The story is told by the adult Michael, looking back on the fateful summer that marked the end of the precarious happiness and fragile way of life they had built.

The Mundy sisters had been able to hold their heads up in a society that frowned on single women. Christina's affair with Gerry had dented their defenses somewhat, but they still clung to the fact that their older brother Jack had become a priest and been sent to Africa to convert the heathen. Having a priest in the family provided status in Ireland's church-dominated society—and having him away "converting the heathen" was especially prestigious. Then came the word that he had been relieved of his duties and was being sent home. The sisters, eager to see him again and looking forward to showing him off proudly to the community, go about preparing the house for his arrival. Michael also is eager to meet his famous uncle.

When they all go to meet him at the bus stop, they are not prepared for the shock of beholding the shadow of a man who emerges from the bus. Gaunt and speaking in a hesitant manner, he is not the Jack whom they had sent off to Africa. They are shocked when they see a number of pagan African artifacts in his luggage. Worse, many of the villagers also see them, including the harsh priest, Kate's boss. Over the next few days they learn that "the heathens" had affected their brother more than he had affected them. He seems a frail, broken man, and yet his once hard, censorious faith, so law-centered and guilt-inducing like Kate's, has softened, allowing the hitherto hidden grace of the faith to emerge.

Matters become more complicated when Christina's long-absent lover Gerry shows up on a motorbike, rekindling her love. Michael stands off from his father at first, but soon melts to the man's many charms. Rose also has attracted a lover, a ne'er-do-well neighbor more after her body than her heart. Kate loses her teaching position, the priest claiming it is due to declining enrollment, but she knows it is because of all the scandal in her family. The rumor that a mill is about to open proves to be true also, which will mean that the sisters' cottage industry of weaving gloves will end. Nor can they expect to find employment at the factory, because the mill owners will hire only younger women. And Gerry dashes Christina's hope of a settled family life with his announcement that he has stopped off but briefly. He soon will be on his way to enlist with the foreign brigade in Spain fighting against Franco's Fascists.

The sisters and Jack express a desire to go to the celebration of the old pagan god Lugh, the god of light. The old harvest festival in the forest is still kept, even by those who attend mass in the churches. Kate will have none of it, forbidding them to attend. It is far too wild and uncontrolled an event for her. Rose sneaks off anyway to meet her lover, and shortly later Jack also sets forth. The wild abandon and lust of the dancers scares Rose, but when she asks to leave, her drunken lover forces her to remain. She manages to get away before coming to harm, but it is not until the next day that she is found by Jack and returned home.

The Scene

Time into film: 1:16:20   Stop at 1:21:07

Later, all five sisters are in the house, some of them listening to the decrepit old radio that Gerry has managed to repair. An Irish country-dance tune comes on, filling the house with its infectious rhythm, even reaching the ears of the men and Michael outside. Maggie, tapping her toe, is the first to give in to the music, getting up and dancing. Rose quickly joins her, then Agnes, followed by Christina. Last of all, Kate gives in to what she normally regards as irreverent foolishness. The five dance around the room and then out the door. Holding hands, the five sisters celebrate the bond of love and sisterhood that has forged them together and sustained them through plenty and want.

The music grows louder, and the dancers more passionate and abandoned. They circle round and around, and at times weave in and out among each other, their now graceful feet seeming barely to touch the ground. Jack watches with open-eyed astonishment: never has he seen his proper sisters give way so to the pleasure of the moment.

Michael and Gerry come up, they too staring in wonder and surprise. The women pay them no heed. Nor do the men try to join in the dance. All seem to realize that this is the sisters' moment. The music and dance rises to a crescendo, and finally come to an end, the dancers standing in their circle in silence. They are physically exhausted, yet emotionally and spiritually charged. As Michael relates in his narrative, it was as if the dance had transported them all, dancers and watchers, into a realm where language no longer existed because words were no longer necessary. The sisters in that joyous moment represent all the women everywhere who had been buffeted and held down by oppressive circumstances, yet who refused to give up hope. This, Michael observes, would be the high point of their lives, some of them going on, with the breakup of the farm, to sad and lonely fates. But this brief, shining moment would remain with them forever, binding their hearts together and promising a far better fate in another world.

Reflection on the Scene

Created in the image of God, we are born to celebrate the goodness of the creation and of the Creator. Many people have much to celebrate in life, while others, such as the impoverished Mundy sisters, have very little. And yet even they find that life is worth celebrating, even in their hardscrabble situation. The ancient temple services, reflected in the last few of the Psalms, must have been joyous occasions, especially for the peasants who lived a hand-to-mouth existence on their little farms. Christianity, too, was a joyful faith, Jesus declaring that he came to make our lives joyful. This was the intention at the very beginning of the gospel story when the angels proclaimed "good tidings of great joy" to the shepherds.

Too often, however, those who make religion into a set of rules and regulations (largely negative) forget this. The Pharisees could not share in Jesus' joy over dining with sinners and seeing them change their ways. In his famous story of the Father and Two Sons the elder brother resents the return of his younger brother so much that he refuses to go into the joyful party thrown by their father to celebrate his return. The early church included dancing, but this gradually was eliminated. The church in Ireland became so sober and guilt inducing that the joy of the faith was covered up. In our story the African pagans do Father Jack a real service by stripping away the gloomy shell of his faith, letting out the joy and light that had been covered up. Give me Father Jack, even in his broken-health state, to the priest that dismisses Kate!

For the last forty years Christians have been loosening up their churches, thanks to such songs as Sidney Carton's "Lord of the Dance" (a.k.a. "I Danced in the Morning") and other folk and praise hymns. One pastor founded the thriving Fellowship of Merry Christians, designed to bring mirth back into the church, and hundreds of pastors and educators followed the lead of Lutheran Floyd Schaefer to become clown ministers. These talented, colorful characters have helped remove the starch from the church's shirts and collars, reminding us that both Sunday and the Lord's Supper are to be celebrated, not endured. The story of the Mundy sisters and their transporting dance is fit to place alongside that of *Zorba the Greek*. Both affirm that life is good, despite the catastrophes that come along. As Christians we believe that Jesus is the Lord of the Dance because neither Pilate nor the cross nor the grave could contain him. He is loose on the earth and invites us all to join him in the dance of life.

For Further Reflection

1. Do you identify with serious-minded Kate, always fussing over others and worried about the rules and

what others will say? What do you dread? What threatens your bliss? Health problems? Finances? What keeps you from being bogged down by these things?

2. Are you more romantically inclined like Christina? Or fun loving like the other sisters? Who in your family or among your friends are like these?

3. What in your life is worth celebrating? What forms do your celebrations take? Have you known the moment of wild abandon experienced by the Mundy sisters? Have you indulged in a water fight or a food-throwing fest and not worried about what the neighbors might think?

4. What signs and moments of joy do you see and experience in your life? How can you and friends add to this?

HYMN: "Joyful, Joyful, We Adore Thee"; "Simple Gifts"; or "I Danced in the Morning"

A Prayer

O God, Creator of all of life, you caused the morning stars to sing together and all the heavenly beings to shout for joy. We praise you for your gift of life and its opportunities. Even in the midst of darkness you cause your light to shine, assuring us of your presence and watch-care. Teach us to dance in the spirit, even when a cross looms before us, assured by your presence that Easter follows Good Friday as surely as the rainbow appears while much of the sky is still dark and threatening. In the name of the Lord of the Dance we pray. Amen.

11. *Dogma*
An Unusual Annunciation

When all the people witnessed the thunder and lightning, the sound of the trumpet, and the mountain smoking, they were afraid and trembled and stood at a distance, and said to Moses, "You speak to us, and we will listen; but do not let God speak to us, or we will die." Moses said to the people, "Do not be afraid; for God has come only to test you and to put the fear of him upon you so that you do not sin." Then the people stood at a distance, while Moses drew near to the thick darkness where God was.

Exodus 20:18–21

In the sixth month the angel Gabriel was sent by God to a town in Galilee called Nazareth, to a virgin engaged to a man whose name was Joseph, of the house of David. The virgin's name was Mary. And he came to her and said, "Greetings, favored one! The Lord is with you." But she was much perplexed by his words and pondered what sort of greeting this might be. The angel said to her, "Do not be afraid, Mary, for you have found favor with God. And now, you will conceive in your womb and bear a son, and you will name him Jesus. He will be great, and will be called the Son of the Most High, and the Lord God will give to him the throne of his ancestor David. He will reign over the house of Jacob forever, and of his kingdom there will be no end." Mary said to the angel, "How can this be, since I am a virgin?" The angel said to her, "The Holy Spirit will come upon you, and the power of the Most High will overshadow you; therefore the child to be

born will be holy; he will be called Son of God.
And now, your relative Elizabeth in her old age
has also conceived a son; and this is the sixth
month for her who was said to be barren. For
nothing will be impossible with God." Then
Mary said, "Here am I, the servant of the Lord;
let it be with me according to your word." Then
the angel departed from her.

Luke 1:26–38

And war broke out in heaven; Michael and his
angels fought against the dragon. The dragon
and his angels fought back, but they were
defeated, and there was no longer any place for
them in heaven. The great dragon was thrown
down, that ancient serpent, who is called the
Devil and Satan, the deceiver of the whole
world—he was thrown done to the earth, and his
angels were thrown down with him.

Revelation 12:7–9

Introduction

The strong street language and the quirky, humorous
approach to religion made this film a difficult one for
older adults to accept. Young adults, however, loved it
and most of them saw that filmmaker Kevin Smith was
not attacking the Catholic Church but rather its
foibles—foibles that Protestant leaders, as well as bish-
ops, sometimes enter into when they try to "improve"
the church. After a funny statement disclaiming any
intention of the filmmakers to disrespect God, the
story begins with a press conference at which the
would-be-hip Cardinal Glick unveils a cutesy "Buddy
Jesus" statue. Sounding more like a Hollywood press
agent than a prelate of the church, Cardinal Glick

states that he intends the winking Jesus, with his hand reaching out in a "thumbs-up position," to replace the crucifix. The dreary traditional symbol of Christianity is, the Cardinal states, outmoded for today's positive age because it is a "wholly depressing image of our Lord, Jesus Christ."

The good cardinal also has arranged with the Vatican for a plenary indulgence to be granted to those who pass through the arched gateway of St. Michael's Church on a certain Friday as part of a church renewal campaign called "Catholicism—Wow!" St. Michael's is located in New Jersey and is about to celebrate an anniversary. Two fallen angels exiled to Wisconsin read about this and see the archway as a means to reenter the heaven out of which they were cast long ago. And so they set out for New Jersey, stopping along the way to resume the work that one of them had once performed for God as the Angel of Death. Now, for reasons best known to God and to Kevin Smith, the removal of guilt and punishment from these two angels would undo creation because their readmission to heaven, guaranteed by the plenary indulgence, would go against God's unchangeable decree that had cast them out of heaven in the first place. So, to save the universe, God sends his Metatron (apparently a herald like Gabriel) to a woman named Bethany to call her forth on a mission to intercept the angels and prevent them from entering the church, thus saving not only Western Civilization but also the whole universe. Whew!

Bethany, we see, is a Catholic who has it in for God. She still attends mass, but because of her messed-up past, she cannot really commit to her Creator. We learn that she had been so in love with her high school sweetheart that they attended the same college, where they roomed together. When she became pregnant, she wanted to abort the baby because otherwise she would have to drop out of college. Her lover objected, suddenly desiring a family. He gave her an ultimatum to have the baby or he would leave her. He knew someone at Planned Parenthood, so Bethany turned instead to a medical student for an abortion, telling her lover that she had miscarried. They graduated and married, but were unable to have a child, the gynecologist telling them that the abortionist tore up her insides. The husband was so upset with this news that he asked her for a divorce. Bethany emerged from this experience convinced that God did not care enough to help her.

The Metatron would have done well to have studied up on the modern American woman, and Bethany in particular. He approaches Bethany in the same way that Gabriel had addressed Mary of Nazareth two millennia earlier. Big mistake.

The Scene

Warning: This has been a controversial film because of its humorous tweaking of the foibles of church leaders and because of its strong street language. The "F" word is spoken several times by the heroine in the scene described below, as well as throughout the film. Those wanting to use this scene, or any part of this film, in a worship service will want to describe the scene rather than show the video clip. A young adult group probably will not be bothered much by the language, but many older adults will be. In any case, if you use the clip with a group, be sure to warn the members ahead of time of what to expect.

Time into film: 0:14:10   Stop at 0:24:11

In what amounts to a funny takeoff on the Annunciation, the Metatron confronts Bethany in her bedroom during the middle of the night, speaking from amidst a sheet of heavenly flame that envelops him. Terrified that she is about to be burned or raped by the intruder, she jumps over to her closet and grabs her home fire extinguisher. The Metatron barely gets out a sentence—"Behold the Metatron, Herald of the Almighty and the Voice of the True God!"—before Bethany douses him with the full contents of the canister. He doubles over, hacking away, as she turns on her lamp. Uttering an Anglo-Saxon expletive, Bethany, armed with a baseball bat, demands to know who he is, warning him that she is calling the police. Now over his shock at her unseemly reaction, the Metatron uses his miraculous powers to still the telephone and turn the woman's bat into a fish. He tells her to shut up, but she is still afraid that he is there to rape her. He reassures her that this is impossible when he reveals that he does not have the equipment for such an act.

He tells her that he is a seraph, in particular the Metatron, whose duty is to be the voice of God. When Bethany asks why God does not speak for Himself (*sic*), he points out, as Moses and the children of Israel knew, that no human could possibly encounter the blazing glory of God and live. Therefore he speaks for God, and his word for her is that God has called her to go to New Jersey on a mission to intercept the two rebellious angels and thus save creation. Bethany continues to be skeptical of the whole enterprise, especially as to why she, a semi-lapsed Catholic working at an abortion clinic, would be chosen. The Metatron uses all his miraculous powers and persuasive arguments to convince her, transporting them to a Mexican restaurant down the street. However, when he leaves, her decision is still very much up in the air. Clearly this is no meek maid from Galilee, obediently declaring, "Here am I, the servant of the Lord; let it be with me according to your word." It requires an incident the next day that almost does result in her being raped before Bethany accepts her calling from God. What follows is one of the funniest religious adventures, or should we use the Metatron's word "crusade," ever to be screened.

Reflection on the Scene

Writer/director Kevin Smith has done his homework, in that the Metatron's explanation of why God sends angels or seraphim to earth corresponds with the Hebrew Scriptures account of why the children of Israel are so afraid of God that they plead with Moses to go and represent them in the divine encounters. Later God tells Moses that he cannot actually see the face of God or he would die, so he orders Moses to hide himself in the cleft of a rock as God passes by. Moses "sees" the back of God, not the blazing "face," and so is saved from being consumed by the burning glory. Likewise, Smith knows well the Annunciation story in the New Testament, but instead of dwelling on parallels between the ancient and modern encounters, he focuses on their differences. And what differences they are, the disillusioned and hurt Bethany being anything but respectful of or obedient to her supernatural visitor. Also, the theme of her unworthiness is very biblical, God almost always calling "undeserving" persons to go forth on divine missions: drunken Noah; greedy, grasping Jacob; the fugitive from justice Moses; the youngest, not the older sons of Jesse (David); a Child born in a stable; a bunch of untutored fisherman; and even the persecutor of the church, Saul, destined to become Paul the Apostle.

So what are we to make of this irreverent episode in such a controversial film? If we can handle its vulgarisms, there is much to learn, as well as enjoy, in this comic adventure of the spirit. First, there is Bethany's feeling that she is an unlikely candidate for a heaven-sent mission. Who would not feel this way in such circumstances? Even if we have not done anything really bad, our very ordinariness might make us feel as she did. Many of us grew up with a Sunday school approach to the Scriptures that teach us about the "Great Heroes of the Bible." This approach is taken in most religious videos aimed at children, or in the adult-oriented films such as *The Ten Commandments* or the TNT film *Jacob*. (The latter film cleans up the character of Jacob so much that he seems hardly the same person that the author of Genesis depicts.) This approach focuses on the acts of the human characters rather than God's saving acts; it forgets that it is God, and not its human characters, who is the only "hero" in the Bible. When Bethany reminds the Metatron that she works in an abortion clinic, the messenger reminds her, "Moses was drunk. Look what he accomplished. . . ." He could have gone on, as I did in the preceding paragraph, to cite other unworthy biblical characters who nonetheless were called to be vessels of divine grace. Who are we to deny this truth for our own lives?

Second, there is Smith's insight that God's word has to be mediated by others. We cannot encounter God as God is. This same truth is elaborated in another delightful spiritual comedy, *Oh God!* when God appears to John Denver's assistant produce department manager in the unlikely form of George Burns, telling him that he has to accommodate Himself to human capabilities of perception. Thus does God accommodate us, if we look back on our lives and reflect on those persons who somehow conveyed God's word to us. Or it might be, as it is for so many, something in nature, such as a red and orange sunset, the star-spangled heavens on an especially clear night, or the many, complex configurations of beauty we encounter in a garden or woods when we look closely and deeply.

Third, the Metatron visits Bethany not just so she can have an uplifting spiritual experience. In the life of faith there is no escape from the world and its troubles, but instead a call for mission. Smith would agree with the author of the Letter of James that faith is a matter of doing, not just of believing. In the case of Bethany, as well as that of so many of her spiritual antecedents in the Bible, it is a dangerous mission fraught with great consequences. We too are often called forth on missions, but because the call is not accompanied by such miraculous occurrences, we might not perceive the phone call or plea from someone for help as a call to mission. I remember years ago praying and thinking about a mimeographed letter that came from the National Council of Churches during the spring, asking ministers to go to Mississippi to be counselors for the young civil rights workers flooding into the state that summer. My wife and I talked it over and prayed about it, and then that Sunday, as we sang in church a hymn about following Christ, we both knew that this was indeed a call. No fire or booming, angelic voice, just a duplicated letter and a Sunday hymn. But a divine call nonetheless.

And so, Kevin Smith, borrowing from the Book of Revelation the ancient story about a war in heaven and drawing on the insights of a Bible with which he apparently is well acquainted, has given us a visual parable that, despite much of its R-rated content, has much to offer the church. But some will turn away, turned off by the language and attitudes of the film's characters. Only those with "eyes that see" will benefit from its spiritual insights.

For Further Reflection

1. Think back on your life and single out one or two persons who have made an impact on your faith. Were any of them an unlikely instrument of God?

2. When have you believed that you were entrusted with a mission? What were the circumstances?

3. What mission do you believe you have now? Is it connected with your church, or perhaps with your job, school, or a club or service organization to which you belong?

4. Check out your church's service of baptism and confirmation. What in the liturgies show that to be a Christian means to be "commissioned"?

HYMN: "The Angel Gabriel From Heaven Came" or "Somebody's Knocking at Your Door"

A Prayer

O God, we marvel at the many ways in which you approach and speak your word to us. You are not a distant deity sitting in heaven and merely observing our hurts and struggles here on earth.

Give eyes to our faith that we might see and hear you, even in the midst of the mundane and routine;

Give courage to our faith, that we might dare to attempt the "impossible";

Give love to our faith that we might reach out
  even to those who have injured us;
Give humility to our faith that we might give
  you, and not ourselves, the credit.
We thank you that even in such unlikely and
  controversial places, such as a movie theater
  showing R-rated films, you are able to speak
  to us. This we pray in Christ's name. Amen.

12. *Entertaining Angels: The Dorothy Day Story*
The Man Who Stayed, and Stayed, for Dinner

Happy are those who consider the poor;
  the LORD delivers them in the day of trouble.
The LORD protects them and keeps them alive;
  they are called happy in the land.
You do not give them up to the will of their enemies.
The LORD sustains them on their sickbed;
  in their illness you heal all their infirmities.

                                    Psalm 41:1–3

He said to his disciples, "Therefore I tell you, do
not worry about your life, what you will eat, or
about your body, what you will wear. For life is
more than food, and the body more than clothing. Consider the ravens: they neither sow nor
reap, they have neither storehouse nor barn, and
yet God feeds them. Of how much more value
are you than the birds! And can any of you by
worrying add a single hour to your span of life?
If then you are not able to do so small a thing as
that, why do you worry about the rest? Consider
the lilies, how they grow: they neither toil nor
spin; yet I tell you, even Solomon in all his glory

was not clothed like one of these. But if God so clothes the grass of the field, which is alive today and tomorrow is thrown into the oven, how much more will he clothe you—you of little faith! And do not keep striving for what you are to eat and what you are to drink, and do not keep worrying. For it is the nations of the world that strive after all these things, and your Father knows that you need them. Instead, strive for his kingdom, and these things will be given to you as well.

"Do not be afraid, little flock, for it is your Father's good pleasure to give you the kingdom. Sell your possessions, and give alms. Make purses for yourselves that do not wear out, an unfailing treasure in heaven, where no thief comes near and no moth destroys. For where your treasure is, there your heart will be also."

Luke 12: 22–34

Let mutual love continue. Do not neglect to show hospitality to strangers, for by doing that some have entertained angels without knowing it.

Hebrews 13:1–2

Introduction

Long before there was a Mother Teresa, Dorothy Day was feeding and sheltering the poor, first of Manhattan, and then, through her newspaper *The Catholic Worker* and the workers' movement that it fostered, the world. This film captures some of the spirit and dedication of this "saint of the streets," and shows how she herself was led to her ministry through circumstances and the forceful efforts of one remarkable man. The film opens with young

Dorothy marching in a suffragette parade during President Wilson's reelection campaign. She becomes embroiled in a fight, makes a friend, goes to work for a Communist newspaper, and hangs out in Greenwich Village with such artists and intellectuals as Eugene O'Neill and John Dos Passos. Telling O'Neill that she wants more out of life than she has found thus far, she falls in and out of love, becomes pregnant and has an abortion, then falls in love with a winsome freethinker named Forster. (Not shown in the film are Dorothy's considerably extended travels to Chicago, Europe, and finally Hollywood to work on a screen adaptation of her novel, from which she earned enough money to buy a small house near the Staten Island seashore.)

Forster is upset when she is attracted to the Catholic Church by a nun who feeds the poor instead of just talking about them. (Dorothy and her radical friends had talked a lot about poverty but had done nothing in a face-to-face way of helping the poor.) Dorothy endures the ridicule of her cynical, sophisticated friends as they trash the church, but she so admires the nun's down-to-earth soup kitchen and friendship with so many of the poor that she decides to join. Even more of a reason is the fact that she is pregnant again. After giving birth to a daughter she names Tamara, she tells Forster during one of their arguments that she wants some stability in their lives. The baptism of Tamara and Dorothy is the final straw that breaks their relationship. Forster stalks off with the cry that he will not be caged.

The movie then jumps ahead several years to the early Depression era. Dorothy and Tamara are walking through a tenement street on their way to the apartment of Dorothy's brother and sister-in-law, John and

Tessa. She has returned to the city to continue her work as a journalist. It pays so little that she must depend on the good graces of her brother and sister-in-law for lodging. She writes numerous, impassioned articles exposing the terrible circumstances of the tenement dwellers, so many of whom are unemployed and thus thrown out into the streets because they cannot pay their rent. The camera effectively shows us their horrible conditions, and in a close-up of Dorothy praying in a church, we feel her anguish over her seeming ineffectiveness to be of much help. She pleads with God to "tell me what you want, what I'm supposed to do." In the very next scene she receives an answer to her prayer, a very unexpected one. (Doesn't God often act in this way?)

The Scene

Time into film: 0:49:57   Stop at 0:58:48

Dorothy returns to the little apartment she and daughter Tamara share with John and Tessa. Tamara jumps into her mother's arms, but brother and sister-in-law seem a little ill at ease. They indicate that someone is waiting to meet her. Dorothy goes to the living room and sees a man sitting in the easy chair, his face hidden by a book. When she greets the guest with a "Hello," he ignores the social niceties and in a voice loaded with a heavy French accent launches into a brief soliloquy: "You know what is wrong with the world? Those who act don't think, and those who think don't act." We soon learn this is the man's customary behavior, so focused is he on his subject.

Dorothy learns that the man is Peter Maurin, directed to her by the editor of the magazine in which some of her stories about the poor had appeared. The ever-polite John and Tessa had invited Peter to stay for supper. As they lay out a plate of chicken and vegetables, Peter attacks it as if he were not sure when or where he would find his next meal. (Later we learn that this is indeed the case, for Peter espouses a life of poverty and is living with the dispossessed on the streets.) The others look on bemusedly at his vociferous stuffing of his mouth. He is a man who obviously enjoys good food, but between mouthfuls he continues philosophizing: "There is no sin in being rich. There is no sin in being poor. But there is a great sin in having more than you need and not sharing it with those who do have less than they need!" Peter finishes his food and continues his speaking, telling Dorothy that she and he together have much to do. Dorothy interrupts him by reminding him that she and her family are hungry. Eat first, talk later.

It is late that same night: Tamara is asleep in the living room with her uncle and aunt. We hear Peter still engaged in his non-stop, one-way conversation with Dorothy. John picks Tamara up to carry her to bed. Now we see Dorothy moving Peter toward the door. He is starting to read from his notebook a copy of "The Prayer of St. Francis," but Dorothy, no longer listening, pushes him through the door as she tells him they will talk another time. The next morning, when Dorothy descends the stairs on her way to work, there is Peter, picking up at the point in the prayer where he left off the night before. They emerge from the subway near the newspaper office where Dorothy works, Peter still haranguing her about the poor. She says that she has to get to work and leaves him on the street. He turns to bystanders and speaks to them. That evening, when Dorothy reemerges, Peter is still preaching to anyone who will listen: "Blessed are the poor. . . ."

Shortly thereafter Dorothy stands in an alley observing Peter address a small crowd of street people. He makes them laugh by telling a joke about a priest and a man. The two exchange glances, and we know that the reluctant Dorothy is won over. Back at her family's apartment Peter tells her, "We don't need to go to Jerusalem or Rome to find God. We can always find Him wherever we are. God is as close as the closest human being, especially the poor." Putting his cap on, he prepares to leave. "Where are you going?" Dorothy asks. His indirect answer, as he goes out the door is "You know Jesus had nothing. The son of a village carpenter, a poor man, and he was followed by poor men. Good night."

Dorothy goes out into the hallway to watch him go down the stairway. John and Tessa come out, hesitantly, even apologetically, suggesting that there is no room for late night guests in their cramped apartment. Peter's here at all times, they complain. Dorothy replies by telling them what she has learned of his background, that he was a French peasant, a Christian Brother, a homesteader in Canada, who owns only the clothes on his back and who slept in the street last night. "He lives with the poor. Hears their voices. He knows the things I need to know. . . ." Understanding the plea in her voice, Tessa supports her sister-in-law as she says, "My mother used to say, 'Take care. You never know when you're entertaining an angel.'"

Reflection on the Scene

Peter Maurin's entrance into Dorothy's life is played for the comic value of the man's single-mindedness and disregard for social graces—a welcome touch in a film seriously concerned about the disparity between the rich and the poor. However, as we listen to Peter Maurin's words and see his influence on Dorothy grow, we realize what a forceful personality he must have been. In the very next scene Dorothy returns to an apartment filled with street people being fed from a kettle of soup simmering on the stove. When Dorothy asks where they came from, her family tells her that Peter brought them. And soon it is Peter who tells Dorothy that she is not going to just write about the poor and feed them in her own home, she is going to launch a newspaper to champion their cause, to provide a voice for those who have suffered in silence for so long.

All through her life, long after his premature death, also depicted in the film, Dorothy gives this man whom she called "the peasant of the pavement" credit for the great influence he exerted on her thought and life. Peter was very much like the saint whose great prayer he read to Dorothy. He took Jesus' words as literally as possible: "Sell your possessions, and give alms. Make purses for yourselves that do not wear out, an unfailing treasure in heaven, where no thief comes near and no moth destroys. For where your treasure is, there your heart will be also." Yet even though he possessed almost nothing himself, he also seems like St. Francis in that he did not expect everyone to live as he did. Peter knew that the rich could not divest themselves of everything, but he did demand that they share, as we heard him say in the film, "There is no sin in being rich. There is no sin in being poor. But there is a great sin in having more than you need and not sharing it with those who do have less than they need!"

Dorothy Day today is much better known than her mentor Peter Maurin. She lived long after him, steering *The Catholic Worker* through crisis after crisis, founding her hospitality houses to shelter and feed people in city after city, and writing and demonstrating for the poor and against war until 1980, the year of her death. The film does us a real service in bringing to light the role of this remarkable man who, through the talented and tenacious Dorothy Day, spread the teaching of His Master that love means feeding and clothing anyone who is in need and not just praying and going to church. As we think about the scenes above we might call to mind the faces of those who have been our mentors in the faith through the years. The same writer who cautioned his readers, "Let mutual love continue. Do not neglect to show hospitality to strangers, for by doing that some have entertained angels without knowing it," also wrote that we are "surrounded by a great cloud of witnesses." Whose names would you add to those of Peter Maurin and Dorothy Day?

For Further Reflection

1. The next time that you are at church, look around at the people there. Who has been an important influence in your faith development? Are they in the choir; teaching at church school; handing out bulletins Sunday after Sunday; the present or past occupant of the pulpit? When did you last let them know how you have been helped by them? Why not now?

2. Do you think the poor are being heard or represented in the media or government? How are most ads and state lotteries almost like a slap in the face of the poor?

3. In what ways is your church helping the poor? What is your role? Are you one of those who, in Peter's words, just think without acting, or act without thinking—or has your reading of Scripture, involvement in church, and watching such films as this one helped you to do both?

HYMN: "Where Cross the Crowded Ways of Life" or "When a Poor One"

A Prayer

The Prayer of St. Francis
Lord, make me an instrument of your peace.
Where there is hatred, let me sow love;
where there is injury, pardon;
where there is doubt, faith;
where there is despair, hope;
where there is darkness, light;
where there is sadness, joy.

O Divine Master, grant that I may not seek so much
to be consoled as to console;
to be understood as to understand;
to be loved as to love.
For it is in giving that we receive;
it is in pardoning that we are pardoned,
and it is in dying that we are born to eternal life.
    Amen.

13. *Erin Brockovich*
Prophet in a Miniskirt

Come, O children, listen to me;
    I will teach you the fear of the LORD.
Which of you desires life,
    and covets many days to enjoy good?
Keep your tongue from evil,
    and your lips from speaking deceit.
Depart from evil, and do good;
    seek peace, and pursue it.

The eyes of the LORD are on the righteous,
    and his ears are open to their cry.
The face of the LORD is against evildoers,
    to cut off the remembrance of them from the
        earth.
When the righteous cry for help, the LORD hears,
    and rescues them from all their troubles.
The LORD is near to the brokenhearted,
    and saves the crushed in spirit.

Many are the afflictions of the righteous,
    but the LORD rescues them from them all.
                                    Psalm 34:11–19

Now large crowds were traveling with him; and
he turned and said to them, "Whoever comes to
me and does not hate father and mother, wife
and children, brothers and sisters, yes, and even
life itself, cannot be my disciple. Whoever does
not carry the cross and follow me cannot be my
disciple."
                                    Luke 14:25–27

Do not be conformed to this world, but be transformed by the renewing of your minds, so that
you may discern what is the will of God—what is
good and acceptable and perfect.

Romans 12:2

"Blessed are those who hunger and thirst for
righteousness, for they will be filled."

Matthew 5:6

Introduction

The apostle Paul would not have had to worry about
Erin Brockovich being "conformed to this world" had
she been a member of his flock. But he would have
rebuked her for her provocative mode of dress—and no
doubt she would have told him where to get off. Erin
likes skimpy skirts, and she does not care what others
think. She should have, for it is her outlandish appear-
ance, and her foul, tart tongue that cause her to lose the
sympathy of the jury and thus what should have been a
sure bet in her lawsuit against the doctor who ran a red
light and plowed into her beat-up car, causing her a
painful neck injury. When the jury rules against her, she
blames her lawyer Ed Masry and is soon at his office
demanding work. With several children to feed and
clothe, she desperately needs a job. She browbeats
Masry into giving her a file clerk position, and while she
is going through a raft of papers involving a huge power
company paying the medical bills for a large number of
people, her curiosity is aroused. Why, she asks Ed, is the
company buying the homes of so many people and also
paying their medical bills? The lawyer gives her permission to go out and ask questions of the homeowners.

Erin discovers a series of sad stories of mysterious illnesses afflicting the people of the community next to the power company. She takes a sample of water to an expert at the nearby university and learns that what the company is dumping into the water system must be the cause of all the ailments afflicting the people. Using her charm to gain access to records at the water authority office, she soon is amassing the evidence linking the power company to the pollution.

Erin has been leaving her three children with a baby-sitter, but when the baby-sitter proves unreliable, the distraught mother is not sure what to do. Her neighbor George comes to her rescue by volunteering to watch the children. A long-haired biker, he works for a while to save up money and then quits for the free time to enjoy his bike. Reluctant at first, Erin agrees when she sees how well he and the children get along. Soon she is so immersed in her research and her interviews of people that she is seldom at home to share in her children's lives. The victims of the company trust Erin because of her honesty, so she soon amasses reams of testimony. Needing the help of a bigger firm, Masry teams up with some snooty high-priced lawyers to handle the workload and pay the mounting expenses of the investigation. These lawyers try to shove Erin aside because they regard her as just a file clerk, but she soon proves that without her, there will be no further progress on the case. The victims trust her and her straightforward talk, not the lawyers in their expensive suits and off-putting manners.

All this involvement takes a toll on Erin's relationship with her eight-year-old son, who resents her missing so many of his school activities. This is the prelude for her confrontation with George.

The Scene

Time into film: 1:23:55   Stop at 1:27:25

Erin comes home, late at night as usual, and George tells her that she has to find a different job or a different guy.

Taken aback, Erin replies, "How can you ask me to do that? This job—for the first time in my life I've got people respecting me. Up in Hinckley I walk into a room, and everybody shuts up to see if I've got something to say. I never had that before—ever! Please don't ask me to give it up."

"What about what your kids are giving up?" he retorts.

"Look," she states, "I'm doing more for my kids than when I was parenting!"

"But what about me?"

"Well, what about you?" she asks, her anger now aroused because a man is pressing her again. "All I ever done was bend my life around what men decided!"

"I'm not them," George fires back, "what more do I have to do to prove that to you?"

"Stay!"

"What for? You got a raise. You can afford day care. You don't need me."

George walks out.

Reflection on the Scene

Erin is torn between two goods—her family and relationship with George, and her mission of helping several hundred hurting people obtain justice from a powerful company that has injured and even killed some of their loved ones. It is a difficult choice, one involving what Jesus would call a cross. He warned his disciples that they would have to sacrifice in order to follow him. His words were purposely stern so that they would sink in. They must "hate" their parents, wives, and children! What a thing to say in a society where obligation to parents was regarded as the primary duty! Jesus' use of hyperbole was intended to shock. It did, and it still does. Our loyalty to him, he boldly asserts, must be so great that by comparison our relationship to our families would pale, seeming like hatred.

Erin, of course, is not consciously following Christ. She is so unfamiliar with Scriptures that she cannot remember Goliath's name when she refers to her battle against the huge power company as a David versus "what's his name" struggle. But she is following in the pathway of Christ and the Hebrew prophets who demanded justice for the poor and the powerless in the name of the God of righteousness. Erin, without consciously knowing it, is an instrument of God, a prophet in a miniskirt doing God's will with such devoted passion that she is willing to allow her family and personal relationships to suffer for the greater good.

But Erin has also experienced, as we see in the video scene, the rewards of serving. The promise of Christ to those who hunger and thirst for righteousness has been fulfilled in her newfound feeling of self-respect and dignity. She has discovered a worthy cause larger than herself and her private interests, one that is worth taking up a cross for. Many people never gain this reward, preferring the comfort of their TV sets and small circle of interests. Erin can serve as an example for all of us that service to others is worth the cost.

For Further Reflection

1. What hard choices have you had to make between duty and self-interest? What price has been extracted? *Note:* Sometimes we become so job-obsessed, consumed with getting ahead, that we identify this with duty, but there is a difference. What is this difference?

2. Take a look at the hours you have in a day. How many do you spend with family (unless you are single and alone); in watching TV, playing golf or other recreation; in church and community activities? What causes at church or in the community could use a willing mind and pair of hands?

3. Think back over those times when you have completed tasks for others. Were there rewards, and if so, what were they? Even in "losing" (giving up time and other pursuits, etc.), what was gained? (I think of the line in St. Francis' famous prayer: "for it is in giving that we receive.")

4. What other persons have you heard about who became unwitting prophets in opposing or exposing corporate crimes? (You might read the 2002 Person of the Year issue of *Time Magazine* that profiled some of these people.) What did their efforts cost them? Would you be willing to pay such a cost?

HYMN: "Come, Labor On" or "Where Cross the Crowded Ways of Life"

A Prayer

Gracious God, you deign to use fallible humans to do your work in this world. Help us to hear and see your call to serve, often in places not of our own choosing; and hearing your voice, help us to set aside our excuses and obey. Your Son promised us both a cross and a reward. Help us to accept both with courage and faith, as with love and humility we offer ourselves to you each day. In the name of the One who came not to be served but to serve, we pray. Amen.

14. *Fiddler on the Roof*
Talking with God

So the men turned from there, and went toward Sodom, while Abraham remained standing before the LORD. Then Abraham came near and said, "Will you indeed sweep away the righteous with the wicked? Suppose there are fifty righteous within the city; will you then sweep away the place and not forgive it for the fifty righteous who are in it? Far be it from you to do such a thing, to slay the righteous with the wicked, so that the righteous fare as the wicked! Far be that from you! Shall not the Judge of all the earth do what is just?" And the LORD said, "If I find at Sodom fifty righteous in the city, I will forgive the whole place for their sake." Abraham answered, "Let me take it upon myself to speak to the Lord, I who am but dust and ashes. Suppose five of the fifty righteous are lacking? Will you destroy the whole city for lack of five?" And he said, "I will not destroy it if I find forty-five there." Again he spoke to him, "Suppose forty . . . if I find thirty there. . . . Suppose twenty are found there. . . . Then he said, "Oh do not let the Lord be angry if I speak just once more. Suppose ten are found there." He answered,

"For the sake of ten I will not destroy it." And the
LORD went his way, when he had finished speaking to Abraham; and Abraham returned to his
place.

Genesis 18:22–33

O LORD, you have searched me and known me.
You know when I sit down and when I rise up;
   you discern my thoughts from far away.
You search out my path and my lying down,
   and are acquainted with all my ways.
Even before a word is on my tongue,
   O LORD, you know it completely.
. . . .
Where can I go from your spirit?
   Or where can I flee from your presence?
If I ascend to heaven, you are there;
   if I make my bed in Sheol, you are there.
If I take the wings of the morning
   and settle at the farthest limits of the sea,
even there your hand shall lead me,
   and your right hand shall hold me fast.
If I say, "Surely the darkness shall cover me,
   and the light around me become night,"
even the darkness is not dark to you;
   the night is as bright as the day,
   for darkness is as light to you.

For it was you who formed my inward parts;
   you knit me together in my mother's womb.
I praise you, for I am fearfully and wonderfully
      made.
   Wonderful are your works;
that I know very well.
   My frame was not hidden from you,
when I was being made in secret,

intricately woven in the depths of the earth.
Your eyes beheld my unformed substance.

Psalm 139:1–4; 7–16a

And going a little farther, he threw himself on
the ground and prayed, "My Father, if it is possible, let this cup pass from me; yet not what I want
but what you want."

Matthew 26:39

Introduction

Based on Sholem Aleichem's Yiddish stories of Tevye
the Dairyman, this adaptation of the long-running
Broadway play is one of director Norman Jewison's
most enjoyable films. Filmed in glorious color with a
large, talented cast, the film is both epic and inti-
mate. This intimacy is shown not just between the
members of Tevye's family, but between Tevye and
his God as well. Tevye is married to Golde, and they
have five daughters, almost all of marriageable age.
He ekes out a living delivering milk around the village and countryside, his cart drawn by the family's
decrepit horse. Yente the matchmaker is trying to
arrange a marriage for their oldest daughter, but
because the family is too poor to provide much of a
dowry, the prospects for a husband are not very
exciting.

The village of Anatevka houses a significant number of Jews in Czarist Russia. There have been no
pogroms emanating from the capital for some time,
so Tevye and his neighbors have lived in peace with
their Christian neighbors—though it is a fragile
peace that could change as quickly as the official
policy.

The play opens with a prologue in which Tevye sets the stage by singing of the tradition that gives his family the stability needed to get by in a difficult world. Then the scene shifts to his home where Golde is receiving Yente the matchmaker, who has come with an offer of marriage. They are interrupted by Motel the tailor who wants to see Golde's daughter Tzeitel, but she sends him away. Golde is not too pleased with Yente's announcement that Lazar Wolfe the butcher is seeking the hand of Tzeitel. She refuses to tell her daughter this when Yente leaves. Tzeitel joins with her sisters in speculating as they sing the joyful song "Matchmaker." And then we switch to Tevye on his return home.

The Scene

Time into film: 0:24:12   Stop at 0:29:45
It has not been a good day for the dairyman. He has had to leave his horse at the blacksmith's because it lost a shoe. Thus, as he is pulling the cart himself, he complains about his situation to God, stating that God must be picking on him in particular. Golde, upon seeing him drawing near the house, interrupts him for a moment, but then his thoughts return to God and his situation. He claims not to be complaining—"After all," he says, "with Your help I'm starving to death"— and God did make a lot of poor people, so it's no shame to be poor, but would it have been so terrible if he had a small fortune? Then he breaks into the song that has delighted so many through the years—"If I Were a Rich Man."

Tevye uses a lot of nonsense words that add to the lightness of his approach, and yet beneath his bantering manner is the yearning of all the poor to leave their poverty behind. He wouldn't have to work hard, he states, and he would build a large showcase of a house. His mansion would have three staircases, one exclusively for ascending, one just for descending, and a third just for show. Thinking like the rural peasant that he is, Tevye declaims that he would have lots of fowl—chicks, turkeys, geese, and ducks—in his yard. Their very noise would proclaim what a wealthy man he is. And Golde would be able to put on weight, her duties being to preside over the cooks and servants as she struts about. His own status would be such that the important men in town would come to consult with him. It would not matter whether his advice was good or bad (note that he, unlike Solomon, does not pray for wisdom). When you are rich, everyone thinks you have knowledge. And, not to neglect the spiritual, Tevye sings that being wealthy he would have the time that he lacks now to pray in the synagogue and discuss the sacred writings "seven hours a day."

Tevye ends the song by asking God directly if it "would spoil some vast, eternal plan" if he were a rich man? But he has little time to reflect on this question, for his neighbors, who have been waiting for him to deliver their milk, descend upon him, each remonstrating that he forgot their order for the Sabbath observance. Such is the lot of a very *un*wealthy dairyman!

Reflection on the Scene

"Be careful what you pray for—your prayer might be answered" is a caution we all need to take to heart. This is especially true in the case of Tevye's prayer that he be a rich man. The dairyman's song-prayer calls to mind also Lord Acton's oft-quoted observation about the corruption of power: money, being a form of power, often corrupts its possessor, and a lot of money (in place of "absolute") might corrupt "absolutely." As we hear Tevye declare what he would do with his wealth, we can see that it would not be a good thing for him if God granted his wish. Tevye the poor man is a far better human being than Tevye the wealthy man would be.

But this is not the main insight to be gained from this scene, as important as it is. What I want to emphasize is the intimacy that exists between the lowly milkman and the One whom he addresses as "Lord, who made the lion and the lamb." Tevye follows in the path of the patriarch Abraham in speaking to God as a close companion. In addressing the Deity he does not use exalted, formal language, but simple words he would use in a conversation with Golde. Like Abraham, who bargains with God over the fate of Sodom and Gomorrah, Tevye's is a very approachable God. Tevye would appreciate the psalmist's sense of awe at the omnipresence of the Creator, and also his feeling of intimacy or closeness with God.

Tevye is just a poor dairyman, but spiritually he is rich, even if he does garble the Scriptures each time he tries to quote them. We would do well to emulate him, seeking to engage our Creator in prayer that is more like a conversation than a one-way stream of requests. There should be spaces between our petitions and thanksgivings, spaces of silence, during which we are listening for God. An old hymn puts it well: "And he walks with me, and he talks with me, along life's narrow way."

For Further Reflection

1. What foolish or unwise thing have you prayed for that a) came about, to your sorrow; or b) was not granted, which you now realize was for the best?

2. What prayers can you first remember from your church services? Were these couched in King James English? How did they make you feel and think about God?

3. Do you still pray in such language? Or have you "loosened up" somewhat? What is the advantage of formal language for prayer? Does it make us more aware of the transcendence, "the otherness" of God? What is the advantage of an informal, conversational approach to God?

4. Is it appropriate to pray for material things and passing concerns? How does Jesus' prayer in the Garden of Gethsemane shed light on this?

HYMN: "Sweet Hour of Prayer" or "What a Friend We Have in Jesus"

A Prayer

Gracious God, you have invited us to come to you in prayer, for you are a God who listens as well as speaks. We thank you for men like Abraham who have accepted your invitation, regarding you as the Divine Conversationalist. Help us in our prayers to listen and to speak with you. Give us ears that hear and eyes that see, that we might know you as our constant companion, in good and ill. This we ask in the name of the One who addressed you as "Abba—Daddy." Amen.

15. *The Fisher King*
Table Grace

Be gracious to me, O God, for people trample on
      me;
   all day long foes oppress me;
my enemies trample on me all day long,
   for many fight against me.
O Most High, when I am afraid,
   I put my trust in you.
In God, whose word I praise,
   in God I trust; I am not afraid;
   what can flesh do to me?

Psalm 56:1–4

. . . but you shall love your neighbor as yourself:
I am the LORD.

Leviticus 19:18b

"Then people will come from east and west,
from north and south, and will eat in the kingdom of God. Indeed, some are last who will be
first, and some are first who will be last."

Luke 13:29–30

Introduction

Jack Lucas was once a well-known radio show host
who loved to abuse verbally his callers. When one of
his abusive calls misfires, sending the deranged caller
off on a murderous spree, Jack loses his job. Along
with it he loses his expensive apartment and lifestyle,
and sinks into alcoholism and self-pity. Then one
eventful night he is saved from some brutal toughs

who are about to set him afire because they think he
is a homeless bum polluting their neighborhood. His
rescuer, Parry, leads a motley band of street people.
Parry considers himself a knight on a quest for the
Holy Grail and thinks that Jack has been sent by the
invisible "Little People" to help him. Jack humors
Parry and later learns that his rescuer was once a
professor of medieval literature. He went over the
edge when his beautiful wife was shot as she sat
across from him at an upscale restaurant. The mur-
derer was the deranged caller for whom Jack's abusive treatment had been the last straw. Up to this
point, Jack had been filled with an amorphous sense
of guilt, though his remorse was centered more on
himself than on his victims. Now he has someone to
focus on. To atone for his past, Jack decides he will
try to help Parry.

Parry is difficult to help. He doesn't want Jack's
proffered money. He gives it away to the first street
person he meets. Noticing that Parry is obsessed
with the time and with getting to a destination, Jack
tags along. Parry spies a young woman exiting an
office building. It is Lydia, the woman of his dreams.
He has so idealized her, in the manner of the
medieval troubadour and knight, that he dare not
approach her, but he follows and adores her from
afar. Jack sees only an excessively clumsy woman,
getting caught in doors and spilling things—but he
determines to help his strange new friend. Enlisting
the help of his own girlfriend, Anne, Jack concocts
an elaborate plan to contact Lydia and trick her into
meeting a spruced-up Parry.

The meeting almost ends in failure, Lydia turning
out to be so insecure that she immediately suspects
anyone showing an interest in her. She would under-

stand the feeling of the psalmist: "for people trample on me; all day long foes oppress me." But when she admires Anne's decorated fingernails and Jack quickly suggests that Anne could do hers, Lydia finally agrees to come to Anne's apartment for a manicure and nail-decorating appointment.

The Scene

Time into film: 1:24:26　Stop at 1:30:45

Down in the street, just outside Anne's apartment, we see Jack and Parry, both decked out as we have not seen them before. Parry is wearing a white suit and dragging his heels, overcome by a sudden attack of shyness. Jack lends him his wallet so that Parry can pay for the meal, and then almost drags his friend up the stairs. When Jack enters the doorway of the apartment, Lydia and Anne are rolling with laughter on the floor. Anne has been able to overcome Lydia's painful reticence during the nail-decorating session. But Lydia reverts immediately to her old shy, hostile self when she spies Jack. She tries to crawl behind the furniture. Jack himself is having difficulty with Parry, who refuses to come out of the hallway. Jack snatches him, holding his arm around him so tightly that Parry has to walk with Jack into the apartment as though they were Siamese twins. Trying to be relaxed, Jack says that they are on their way to supper and invites the women to come along. Anne says yes, but Lydia refuses. After a brief but furious exchange between the two women, Anne, far more forceful than her meek guest, says that they will come.

In the street Parry walks with Lydia and tries to engage her in small talk. She describes her work at a publishing house, denying Parry's attempt to assign importance to it. He refuses to accept her self-put-downs.

When she says that most of the books she evaluates are just trashy romance novels, Parry picks up from a trash can the wire and tinfoil top of a champagne bottle and quietly works with the debris as he tries to convince Lydia of the worth of her work. Declaring that there is nothing trashy about romance, he presents to her the tiny chair he has fashioned from the cast-off material. Lydia for the first time is impressed.

The four are seated in a garishly decorated booth of a Chinese restaurant. Lydia is hopeless with chopsticks. Parry is more adept, but as she drops food on the floor, he deliberately drops some too. One morsel of food seems to run away of its own will from her pursuing chopsticks. So does Parry's. She spills a drink, and he, to set her at ease, does so also. Jack and Anne look on with mild horror and fascination. They were made for each other, Anne whispers to Jack.

Gradually, as Parry mirrors her clumsy antics, Lydia's reserve and hostility melts away. Probably for the first time in years she feels at ease with someone, someone who seems as inept and klutzy as herself. She snorts and makes other little animal sounds, showing that now she is thoroughly enjoying the evening. Parry himself seems a different person. During their walk to the restaurant, we hear little of the mad Parry with his talk of mythical little people and a search for the Holy Grail. Instead, he is more like the professor that he was, alert and lucid in his concern to put Lydia at ease. By the end of the meal he has won over Lydia—almost.

Reflection on the Scene

The restaurant scene is a wonderful parable of grace, the kind of grace that we see in the many encounters between Jesus and the outcasts of his day. That table in the Chinese restaurant has become a table of grace, thanks to the loving concern of Parry for Lydia. Parry's love has brought a period of sanity to the man who has thought that he is a knight on a quest, even if he still must be protected by his amnesia from the horror of that night when his wife was murdered. At the same time, his gracious acts at the supper table uncover the beautiful nature of Lydia, obscured by her self-deprecating mind-set and actions. She begins to see herself not through her own disapproving eyes, but through the eyes of one who loves and values her. This is what love does for another person, what is implicit in the ancient commandment to love your neighbor as yourself. Implicit in that commandment is a necessary love for oneself, perhaps best summed up in the overworked term "self-esteem." Parry's love is the beginning of what might be a long process for the woman who esteems herself so lowly and undeserving. Were she to sing "Amazing grace, so rich so free, that saved a wretch like me," her emphasis would have been so much on *wretch* that she would have missed the grace.

It would be pointless to guess why or how Lydia became the way she is when Parry first spies her (our fascination with psychology tempts us to provide what actors call a back story for her). What is important is that we see the wonderfully transforming power of grace in this little scene. This table of grace bears a great resemblance to the Lord's Table to which the secure and the insecure, the richly endowed and those who feel they have nothing, are invited. Both that table smeared with spilled Chinese food and the Table on which sit bread and wine are foretastes of the eating and drinking in the kingdom of God announced by Jesus in Luke's Gospel. Our Lord added a note that especially pertains to Lydia when he declared that "some are last who will be first"—and who at her office has stood more times at the back of the line than she?—"and some are first who will be last."

For Further Reflection

1. With whom do you identify most in the story: Lydia, Parry, Anne, or Jack? If you have wrestled with a sense of not being worthy, how have you dealt with it? Christians believe that our "worthiness" is bestowed on us at baptism, when we are declared a "child of God." How can this help a person develop a sense of self-worth?

2. What do you think of Parry's mirroring of Lydia's clumsiness? What prevents it from becoming parody or mockery? How is this an act of grace instead?

3. We often speak of a gracious host or hostess: what is it that makes a person such? What gracious incidents have you experienced when you were a guest?

4. What can you do to be a person of grace? Or is it more a matter of accepting divine grace than in doing? Look up and read Thomas Toke Lynch's hymn "Gracious Spirit, Dwell with Me." Try using it as a prayer at the beginning of each day for a week or more. (Note that this worthy hymn is not in every hymnal. You can find it in the old red Presbyterian *Hymnbook*.)

5. The psalmist probably was experiencing greater problems than Lydia yet found a sense of security in God. How have you found your faith in God similarly rewarded? What crises have you gone into feeling alone, and then, when you prayed and read Scripture,

found that you were not alone but were upheld by a Power beyond your own?

HYMN: "Gracious Spirit, Dwell With Me" or "God of Compassion, In Mercy Befriend Us"

A Prayer

Gracious God, as the hymn goes, we would indeed seek to be as gracious as your Son, who set all people, even outcasts and sinners, at ease whenever he encountered them. We thank you that even in the fiction of a film we see examples of your grace. Continue, by your Spirit, to work on us, calling us away from our self-centeredness to that Way which, centered on you, leads us to forget our own needs as we minister to the needs of others. We thank you for grace received from others, and pray that we might pass it on to those whom we meet, thereby creating an endless chain of grace foreshadowing the coming of your kingdom. In the name of the One who is the very embodiment of grace, even Jesus Christ our Lord. Amen.

16. *Fried Green Tomatoes*
The Power of Story

> But the thing that David had done displeased the LORD, and the LORD sent Nathan to David. He came to him, and said to him, "There were two men in a certain city, the one rich, and the other poor. . . ."
>
> 2 Samuel 11:27b–12:1

> When Israel went out from Egypt,
>   the house of Jacob from a people of strange language,

Judah became God's sanctuary,
   Israel his dominion.

The sea looked and fled;
   Jordan turned back.
The mountains skipped like rams,
   the hills like lambs.

Psalm 114:1–4

Now all the tax collectors and sinners were coming near to listen to him. And the Pharisees and
the scribes were grumbling and saying, "This fellow welcomes sinners and eats with them." So he
told them this parable: "Which one of you. . . ."

Luke 15:1–3a

Introduction

Evelyn Couch is one of those put-upon persons who
has always done what her husband Ed says. She seems
to find solace in always eating sweets, which of course
causes her weight problem. On the day that she and Ed
make their first visit to his aunt at a nursing home
something happens that will change her life. Ed's aunt
is so crotchety that she runs Evelyn out of her room.
When the rejected woman retires to the home's parlor
to wait for her husband, she meets a talkative elderly
woman. Ninny Threadgoode comes over to introduce
herself in the hope of finding a willing ear for her story
about long-gone times and Idgie Threadgoode.
Evelyn is hooked when Ninny begins by mentioning
Idgie was accused of murder. Who could resist hearing
the details of a story with such a beginning?

Ninny begins with what happened on the day that
Idgie gained a friend and lost a brother. Idgie was a
child then who worshiped her slightly older brother

Buddy. She was a hellion of a tomboy whom only
Buddy could talk into doing something she didn't want
to. On that day it was to put on a dress for her sister's
wedding. Rebellious Idgie tears off the hated clothing
and climbs up to her tree house. Buddy follows her up
into the tree and mollifies her with a story about how
God created oysters and one day made one different by
planting a grain of sand in it. The oyster, he indicates,
is like Idgie, the product of pain and trouble, but beautiful. Later that day the two are introduced to Ruth.
About Buddy's age, Ruth takes a liking to Idgie as well
as Buddy. As they walk along a small dam, Buddy tells
them both another story. When they walk along a
bridge that crosses over the train tracks, the wind
blows Ruth's hat down onto the tracks. Buddy runs to
retrieve it. He finally catches up to it. As he waves it tri-
umphantly, he does not realize that his foot has been
caught between the main rail and one that leads off to
a siding. He hears the whistle of an approaching train
but cannot get away. He frantically tries to unloosen
the lace of his hightop shoe, but there is not enough
time. The train runs over him.

The story continues years later during the
Depression. Idgie has grown up half-wild, dressed
mainly in men's clothing and hanging out at the local
juke joint where she plays cards and carouses the night
away. Her mother brings Ruth back to town in the
hope that she will have a good influence on her recal-
citrant daughter. Ruth, a churchgoer, is soon active in
the local church. Idgie tries to dodge her at first, but
Ruth persists. She is a believer but not a prissy one. She
hangs out with Idgie, even joining her when she climbs
into a boxcar. Ruth is appalled at first, when the slow
moving train passes a Hooverville and Idgie starts
throwing out the cans of food stacked inside to the

hungry people. Soon, however, she too is passing as many cans as she can to the willing recipients running alongside. After this she and Idgie are fast friends. The friendship is interrupted for a few years when Ruth leaves town and returns to Georgia to marry. Idgie had refused to go to the wedding or to visit her erstwhile friend. But, hearing tales that Ruth was being abused, one day she did venture forth to see her. Ruth was reluctant to let her in the house out of fear of what her husband would do. Soon after, Idgie and two friends go and rescue Ruth, bringing her back to Alabama. There Idgie's father borrows money and sets the two women up to open and run the Whistle Stop Cafe, where the chief dishes are fried green tomatoes and barbecued meat.

Ninny tells her story in sections interspersed between present happenings. We see how Ed ignores Evelyn and takes her meals and attempts at rekindling their romance for granted. He prefers televised sports to conversing with her. Evelyn has been attending a women's self-improvement program, but it offers little help. She fantasizes about a Wonder Woman-type heroine whom she dubs Towanda, who is the very opposite of what she is. Even strangers take advantage of her. Two teenagers insult her at the grocery store. She breaks down and cries during her next visit to the home. Evelyn has found that her visits have become a high point for both her life and for the lonely Ninny's.

Ninny continues to relate the fascinating details in Idgie's and Ruth's lives. Ruth had been in the early stage of pregnancy when she was rescued by her friends. She delivers a baby boy and continues to work with Idgie at the Whistle Stop Cafe, a haven for the poor—hoboes and blacks—as well as for the locals, drawn by the delicious barbecues and fried green tomatoes. Ruth's husband Frank hears that he has a son. A member of the Ku Klux Klan, Frank and his friends come at night in sheets and hoods to threaten Ruth and terrorize her black friends. Fortunately Grady, the local constable, is on hand to make them leave. Frank vows to come back and retrieve his son. He returns while Ruth is away and is killed under mysterious circumstances, his actual death witnessed by just two people. Idgie helps to dispose of the body in a grisly but creative way. Ruth returns, unaware of what has happened, other than the fact that Frank had tried to take away her baby, but had left. Idgie assures her that he will never bother her again.

The Scene

Time into film: 1:17:50   Stop at 1:21:55

Evelyn has been mesmerized by Ninny's stories. She has come to admire Idgie's pluck. Idgie's refusal to accept things as they are begins to rub off on her, and Evelyn starts to stand up to Ed. At the grocery store where she had been reduced to tears by the two teenagers, she has an encounter in the parking lot that becomes the turning point in her relations to others who would demean her. Evelyn is in her car waiting for another car to back out of a parking space in the parking lot. Before she can pull into it, a red VW driven by two young women quickly darts in. Evelyn tells them that she had been waiting for that space. The women laugh at her, one of them saying, "Face it, we're younger and faster!" They walk on into the store.

Evelyn sits there in her car for a moment. We can

almost hear her mind saying, "Idgie would never tolerate this!" She smiles and guns the motor. Tires squeal-
ing, she smashes into the back of the offending car.
Backing up, she rams it again, and again. There is not
rage on her face but a happy smile, and then laughter—the laughter of the liberated, of one who has
taken all she can and now is fighting back. The sound
of the repeated ramming brings her two tormentors
out of the store. The smug looks on their faces have
been replaced by consternation. When one protests,
Evelyn calls back, "Face it, girls! I'm older and have
more insurance!" At the home Evelyn now has her
own story to relate to the delighted Ninny. As they
walk through the hall of the home, Evelyn excitedly
exclaims, "I got mad, and it felt good!" She invokes the
name of her fantasy alter ego, "Towanda, Righter of
Wrongs! Queen beyond compare!" The amused
Ninny asks, "How many of them hormones are you
taking, honey?"

Back at her own home Evelyn is exercising as Ed
asks her how she could accidentally hit a car *six times*.
He complains about the diet supper and snack she has
laid out for him, but she ignores his protest. As subse-
quent scenes show, Ed is going to have to adjust to a
new relationship with his wife. From now on Evelyn
refuses to kowtow to Ed's self-centered whims and
wishes. She has become the embodiment of Towanda,
Queen beyond compare.

Reflection on the Scene

As children, one of our frequent requests probably was
"Tell me a story." Seldom does anyone outgrow this
desire. Stories not only relieve present boredom or dis-
satisfaction; they also offer us new ideas and ways of

coping. They draw on the power of our imaginations to transport us to new realms and situations that challenge our tired spirits. Stories of past glory sustain individuals and nations during trying times and enhance the enjoyment of the good times. We see this in the Scriptures wherein the psalmist often rehearses the past acts of God in saving or forgiving Israel. The prophet Nathan uses a story to bring home to King David the enormity of the crime he has committed in seducing Bathsheba and arranging for the death of her husband. A direct attack on the king would have accomplished little, sending David into a defensive attitude. But the simple story of the two men and the little pet lamb captures David's attention and his conscience and leads to a self-condemnation harsher than anything that Nathan could have said. A thousand years later Jesus proved himself a master storyteller by couching so much of his teaching about the kingdom of God in the form of stories that challenged the status quo. When his enemies attack him for spending so much time in the company of the wrong people, Jesus does not fight back directly. Instead, he tells three stories of the lost and the found, trusting that his accusers will get the point.

In our film Evelyn is drawn out of herself by the stories spun by Ninny Threadgoode. For a time she enters into the world of Idgie and Ruth and the denizens of the Whistle Stop Cafe. Fifty years have passed, and the little village by the railroad tracks has fallen into decay, but it all comes alive again when Ninny recalls the exploits of the two women and their friends. And just as Idgie affects her timid friend Ruth, so Ninny begins to have an affect on the hapless Evelyn. Stuck in what seems to be a dead-end situation, Idgie's story helps Evelyn see that there are other connecting streets that she could take. Awakened to new possibilities, Evelyn finds that Idgie's courage is contagious. She stands up to the two women who abuse her in the parking lot in the only way that she can discover at the time. The worm turns, with a power terrible to behold. At home she stands up to Ed, not just over the matter of the parking lot incident but in other areas as well. She refuses to accept his neglect, and when she decides that Ninny should come and live with them, she shows that she means business by taking a sledge and knocking out one of the walls of their house.

This film can inspire us to look at the stories that we have cherished and that perhaps have influenced us more than we realize. It can also help us look at the story of our own lives, at what elements we want to pass on to those who come after us. We too have stories that can inspire and amuse and that can transmit our values to those whom we cherish. In every such story of love and grace and sacrifice, God is to be found, even if not named.

For Further Reflection

1. Was there a story time in your home when you were a child? What stories were read or told to you? Which ones do you remember to this day? What do you think you gained from them, beyond the satisfaction of the moment? If you are a parent, do you provide such a time for your child(ren)?

2. What stories of your family have been preserved and retold down through the years? What do they reveal about your family and its values? How have they made you feel about your family?

3. What stories do you remember from church

when you were a child? What biblical stories were especially emphasized? How have these influenced the church—and you? Has your attitude toward some of them changed? In particular, think about the patriarchal stories–were Sarah and the other women given much attention? David and Goliath—do you still glory as much in the bloody denouement of the story?

4. Which of the stories of Jesus were highlighted? Was much made of his relationship with and attitude toward women and their roles?

5. Compare Jesus' use of parables with his accusers with the incident of Nathan and King David. How is the indirect approach of story better than a discursive, accusatory approach? (See this same approach in Hamlet's play within a play as he captures the conscience of the king.) What is the power of story that appeals to us?

HYMN: "Tell Me the Old, Old Story"

A Prayer

Gracious God, we thank you for our heritage of stories, both those in the Bible that celebrate your mighty acts of salvation and grace, and those from our own families that reveal something of where we came from and who we are. Help us especially to listen to the story of your Son and to enter into its power to challenge and transform us. We thank you, too, for the storytellers of our time, for novelists and filmmakers, who transport us to other times and places where we are also challenged and transformed. May we live out our stories in such ways that they will become a part of your Story, the acts of our lives serving to inspire those to come to live more loving and fruitful lives. We ask

this in the name of the great Storyteller, even Jesus
Christ, our Lord. Amen.

17. *Gandhi*
Turning the Other Cheek—Reality or Metaphor?

> A soft answer turns away wrath, but a harsh word
> stirs up anger.
>
> Proverbs 15:1

> "But I tell you not to try to get even with a per-
> son who has done something to you. When
> someone slaps your right cheek, turn and let that
> person slap your other cheek."
>
> Matthew 5:39 (CEV)

> Bless those who persecute you; bless and do not
> curse them. . . . Do not repay anyone evil for evil,
> but take thought for what is noble in the sight of
> all. If it is possible, so far as it depends on you,
> live peaceably with all. Beloved, never avenge
> yourselves, but leave room for the wrath of God;
> for it is written, "Vengeance is mine, I will repay,
> says the Lord." No, "if your enemies are hungry,
> feed them; if they are thirsty, give them some-
> thing to drink; for by doing this you will heap
> burning coals on their heads." Do not be over-
> come by evil, but overcome evil with good.
>
> Romans 12:14, 17–21

Introduction

Richard Attenborough's *Gandhi* presents in a memo-
rable way the highlights of the life of the great Indian
leader, from his early years in South Africa where he
aspired to be a good English barrister, to the long years

in India where he identified with the poorest of the poor. The film begins with the traumatic event that changed the course of Gandhi's life. Having just arrived in South Africa to represent an Indian businessman engaged in a legal dispute, Gandhi had purchased a first-class train ticket. When a white passenger complained of the presence of an undesirable in the car, the conductor attempted to move the "colored" man to a lower-class car. Gandhi refused, and he was kicked off the train in the dead of night. He finally arrived at his destination and was appalled that his new friends accepted such treatment as a matter of course.

Determined to do something about the unjust laws, which included the requirement that all Indians and blacks must carry a pass whenever they went out, Gandhi announced that he would burn his pass as an act of defiance. He did so in the presence of a white policeman, who, when Gandhi refused to obey his orders to stop burning his pass, beat him with his staff.

At a large public meeting Gandhi vowed to fight the unjust system with nonviolent tactics. Thousands of Indians, who had come to South Africa as indentured servants and tradesmen, flocked to his standard. A movement dedicated to nonviolent political change had been born. The newspapers spread the story of Gandhi and his unorthodox campaign of resistance. The reports attracted an Englishman, curious and concerned about what seemed to be a new way of dealing with large-scale conflict.

The Scene

Time into film: 0:17:10   Stop at 0:20:35

The Englishman is Charlie Andrews, a collar-wearing clergyman. Charlie shows up one day at

Gandhi's home unannounced. Gandhi invites him to walk with him as he proceeds to his office. As they go down a street, they see a group of tough-looking young whites standing around. The men glare at the pair and make some threatening remarks. Charlie suggests that they take an alternate route. No, Gandhi replies, we will go right on. Charlie demurs, and Gandhi asks if Jesus didn't say that we should turn the other cheek when attacked. His companion replies that he thinks Jesus meant it metaphorically. I think not, Gandhi answers, and keeps right on walking toward the toughs. He looks them square in the eye, refusing to get off the sidewalk as one of them commands. The tense situation is defused by the mother of one of them who yells down from the balcony to get on to work. Gandhi says that they will see that there is room for them all, and continues to walk on. He tells Charlie that he believes in the power of nonviolence, that it reaches and activates some good deep within an aggressor.

Reflection on the Scene

Most Christians have agreed with Charlie concerning Jesus' teaching about dealing with an attacker. Even those called fundamentalists, who supposedly take the Scriptures literally, ignore or explain away this difficult passage in their support of "just" wars and capital punishment. How ironic that a Hindu should not only take these words of Jesus literally in interpersonal relationships but also forge a method for dealing with conflict on a massive scale in the struggle of his people to free themselves from the occupying British power. The film scene ends without revealing what happened. We know from Gandhi's previous encounter with the

South African policeman who beat him that he would have faced the toughs with courage and resolution. Maybe his calm courage in facing them was enough in itself. It often is, for bullies depend on their victim's fear to intimidate them. Later Charlie returns with Gandhi to India, becoming a firm believer in Gandhi's philosophy and tactics and writing several books advocating nonviolence.

To watch the film *Gandhi*, or to read in the Sermon on the Mount Jesus' words concerning love and enemies, inevitably brings us face to face with ourselves—how are we to deal with hostility, that of an external enemy and that within ourselves engendered by hostile mistreatment? If we stand up for a principle or stand with someone being mistreated or oppressed, we shall encounter hostility. And even if we accept Jesus' words of absorbing an enemy's blow—striking a person on the right cheek was considered especially insulting in Jesus' time—how are we to deal with the flood of feelings (anger, humiliation, resentment, the burning desire to get even) that well up within us, blocking the path to do what our Master bids us do?

Most Christians admit that, although they can do most of what Jesus commands, the matter of loving enemies is the last, seemingly insurmountable obstacle to living a full "Christian" life. I have always remembered Ernest Gordon's observations in his moving account of coming to accept Christ during his years in a Japanese prisoner of war camp. In *Through the Valley of the Kwai*, Gordon relates that the words about forgiving others stuck in his throat whenever he thought of their Japanese captors. The prisoners had been mistreated far too brutally for them to glibly forgive them. Gordon reports that only after long struggle and striving to understand their captors were the prisoners able to pray *all* of the Lord's Prayer.

What seems like an impossible command—to pray for one's persecutors and to absorb their hostility without retaliating—is explained away, with many people saying that to follow Jesus' words would turn us into doormats, allowing opponents to run over us and to continue with their evil doings. And yet when we look at the history of the early Christians who followed Jesus' path of nonviolence, and also that of Gandhi as he fought the British, we have to admit that they were anything but doormats. We see working in them the power of love, stronger than the hostility of their oppressors. They have learned that when they give themselves over to that power, they are transformed in unexpected ways, enabling them to do the impossible.

What is impossible for us—to control or purge away the hostility within ourselves when we are attacked—becomes possible because of the transforming power of God. In the apostle Paul's midrash on his Master's teachings, Paul not only repeats the teachings of Christ on love and refraining from retaliating, but he goes on to suggest that such behavior will affect the aggressor in a positive way. Quoting from Proverbs 25:21–22, he suggests that by refusing to "cooperate" with the aggressor by returning hostility for hostility, we will appeal to the conscience of the enemy ("burning coals on his head"), perhaps leading to an end of the conflict. The love of Christ, flowing through us, leads to two transformations—that of ourselves and that of our enemy.

For Further Reflection

1. Have you tended to agree with Charlie or with Gandhi with regard to Jesus' words about turning the

other cheek? How does our culture in general seem to regard this statement? What icons do our children and youth look up to—Rambo or Jesus?

2. How do you feel when someone attacks you, either in words or physically? Do you think it is better to deny such feelings or to admit them? By admitting them have you then been able to pray about them, as well as for your opponent?

3. Can you recall times when you or someone you know used the "soft word" of the Proverb in a conflict? You probably can recall a time of returning insult with insult, angry retort with angry retort. Did this quench or kindle the fires of anger and resentment? When the "soft word" was given, what happened?

4. Think of someone with whom you disagree or with whom you share a mutual dislike. Work out a campaign to repair the broken relationship by doing what the Master and the apostle urge us to do. Pray for yourself and for the person. Look for opportunities to say a good word for and to the person. Look for ways of doing something that will help the person and bring about a better understanding between the two of you. Read biographies of those such as Gandhi, Martin Luther King Jr., Francis of Assisi, John Wesley, George Fox, or Dorothy Day, who have been able to love enemies and overcome walls of hostility. Ask fellow Christians to pray for you both. Seek their advice; see if you can discuss the situation without revealing something embarrassing to one or both of you. Read and reread the Sermon on the Mount and chapter 12 of Romans.

HYMNS: "Turn Back, O Man, Forswear Thy Foolish Ways"; "In Christ There Is No East or West"; "When Will People Cease Their Fighting?"

A Prayer

Dear God, you are the Creator of us all, yet we sometimes fail to see the kinship with others. We know we are to live peaceably with everyone, but we cannot always do this. When we enter into conflict, help us to see the humanity within our enemy and the kinship we have because of you. Save us from expressing angry thoughts and cruel intentions of revenge when we are wronged. Give us Christ's spirit of love and forgiveness, even as we seek your forgiveness for ourselves. Bring us to a mature, compassionate understanding of ourselves and of our enemy, and when we can see no way out of an impasse, show us your way of truth and love. We ask this for the sake of your Peaceable Kingdom. Amen.

18. *Harry Potter and the Sorcerer's Stone*
Protected by Love

Blessed be the LORD,
> for he has wondrously shown his steadfast love
> > to me
> when I was beset as a city under siege.
I had said in my alarm,
> "I am driven far from your sight."
But you heard my supplications
> when I cried out to you for help.

Psalm 31:21–22

Beloved, let us love one another, because love is from God; everyone who loves is born of God and knows God. Whoever does not love does not know God, for God is love. God's love was revealed among us in this way: God sent his only

Son into the world so that we might live through him. In this is love, not that we loved God but that he loved us and sent his Son to be the atoning sacrifice for our sins. Beloved, since God loved us so much, we also ought to love one another. No one has ever seen God; if we love one another, God lives in us, and his love is perfected in us.

1 John 4:7–12

Or do you not know that your body is a temple of the Holy Spirit within you, which you have from God, and that you are not your own? For you were bought with a price. . . .

1 Corinthians 6:19–20

Introduction

The Harry Potter books have been a sensational success, and not just with children and youth. Many adult Muggles have delighted in the way that the books and now the fine film adaptation have reconnected them with some of the joy and wonder of growing up. Despite the negative clamoring of some who see only evil in J. K. Rowling's work (I'm reminded of the line from Sidney Carter's great hymn "Lord of the Dance": "I danced for the scribe and the Pharisee, but they would not dance, and they would not follow me. . . ."), most of us find the books and film not only entertaining, but inspiring as well. Young Harry's adventures during his first year at Hogwarts lead him well along the road to maturity, and many of the lessons that he learns are parallel to those taught in the Gospels. The film looks at the world squarely in the eye and sees that there is much suffering and evil—the wizard Voldemort murdered both of Harry's parents, and

Harry himself is in grave danger. There are temptations to overcome and dangers to avoid or to face that require faith and courage. The latter show that there is also good in the world, and above all, as we see in the scene below, there is love, love that is stronger than hate, so that those who choose it will in the end triumph over all the forces of evil.

The Cinderella-like plot involves a boy raised by a hateful aunt and uncle who discovers that he was the child of two wizards who had been killed by the evil Lord Voldemort. Harry, then a baby, was himself almost killed. But he had survived, bearing on his forehead a lightning-shaped scar caused by the encounter. His aunt and uncle, despising his parents, had kept Harry's past a secret and treated him badly. The unhappy boy is mysteriously whisked away to Hogwarts, a school for wizards, where he finds two good friends and an implacable enemy. There are a series of adventures whirling around the quest for the Sorcerer's Stone, which grants its owner almost infinite power over the world. Harry learns that the evil Voldemort, wounded in the incident that had killed Harry's parents, has been slowly regaining his power and is out to obtain the Stone. In the climactic battle with Professor Quirrell, one of his teachers whose body had been taken over by Voldemort, Harry emerges triumphant but seriously wounded, lying unconscious on the floor with the Stone in his hand.

The Scene

Time into film: 2:14:02   Stop at 2:16:18

After his climactic confrontation with Quirrell/Voldemort, Harry wakes up in the sick bay of Hogwarts. He is bruised and battered, but very much alive.

Soon he is joined by kindly Dumbledore. Harry cannot remember all that happened, so the wizard reveals what had transpired, stating that the sought-after Sorcerer's Stone has been destroyed. Harry had been able to obtain it only because he, unlike Voldemort, had not intended to use it ("Blessed are the pure in heart"?). Then Dumbledore asks Harry if he knows why Quirrell had not been able to hold onto Harry during the struggle. "It was because of your mother," Dumbledore explains. "She sacrificed herself for you, and that kind of act leaves a mark." Harry's bandaged hand reaches up to the mark on his forehead. "Oh no," Dumbledore continues, "this is the kind of mark that cannot be seen. It lives in your very skin. What is it? Love, Harry—love."

Reflection on the Scene

How anyone can watch this scene and declare that the film and book are evil is beyond me. In this scene author J. K. Rowling has cut to the heart of the gospel—"God is love." True, she employs no God-talk, so an agnostic or atheist can also appreciate the scene, but for the Christian, the gospel is surely embedded in this entertaining story—and we can only pity those who cannot, or will not, see it because they are put off by the fantasy world in which both science and magic coexist.

The headmaster's words must have helped Harry come to terms with his terrible loss. The longing for his parents' presence will always cause his heart to ache, but knowledge of the wonderful heritage left by his mother will be with him forever. It has already saved his life, and will serve as a guide and inspiration to him for the rest of his days. Harry's story is similar to that chronicled in another book and movie, *Eleni*. Nick, a *New York Times* reporter, returns to his native Greece to try to discover by whom and how his mother was killed during the Communist insurgency there just after World War II. Tracking down various witnesses and returning to his native village high up in the mountains, the reporter finally meets the man who had judged his mother and ordered her execution. In the eyes of the Communist leader, Eleni had been guilty of sending Nick, his sisters, and a group of other children away from the guerilla-occupied village one night to prevent their being sent away to a supposedly safe Communist nation. Eleni herself had been unable to go with the children and other adults because she had been unexpectedly drafted for a work detail. When the guerillas discovered the escape and Eleni's complicity in it, she and several others were arrested, tortured, and sentenced to death. As she faced the firing squad her last words were a defiant cry, "My children!" When Nick goes to meet the former guerilla, he takes a pistol with him, fully intending to extract vengeance. He confronts the man and points the gun at him, but then the man's little daughter enters the room, and Nick cannot bring himself to shoot. Later, on the plane returning home, Nick writes his wife that it is because of his mother that he could not kill. To do so would have denied the heritage of love she had left him. Nick is the kind of man that young Harry probably will grow up to be, a sensitive person forever shaped by the defiant love of his mother.

Fortunate are those such as Harry and Nick who possess such an inheritance of love. They have the gospel in the flesh. As the author of 1 John wrote, "God is love. God's love was revealed among us in this way: God sent his only Son into the world so that we might live through him. In this is love, not that we loved God but that he loved us and sent his Son to be the atoning sacrifice for our sins." The apostle Paul reminds the Corinthians of this heritage when he advises them to keep their bodies pure and tells them that they "were bought with a price," namely, the life of Jesus Christ on the cross.

We too are graced with this inheritance of love, and we bear the mark of love on our bodies. Unlike Harry's lightning scar (which *is* a visible mark resulting from hate thwarted by love!), it is not visible, but it was placed there at our baptism. Many ministers trace with their wet hand or fingers the sign of the cross on the candidate's head to symbolize that it is Christ and his cross that makes possible our entrance into the covenant people of God—and the sign made in water also symbolizes that the baptized is some day to take up a cross and follow Christ.

For Further Reflection

1. Whose love from your past has gotten into "your skin"? Reflect on the person(s) for a few moments. Try to recall an instance in which you experienced that love. Then say a prayer of thanksgiving for that person. (If she or he is still alive, what can you say or do to acknowledge your gratitude?)

2. How else have you experienced the love of God at some specific moment of your life? Do the psalmist's words above express how you have felt?

3. There is a tender scene in the film *Monsoon Wedding* in which the father looks in on his sleeping, grown daughters and says to his wife that he loves them so much he almost feels like bursting. Can you

imagine God looking down on us like that? How is your family, or your relationship with friends if you have no family, like that?

4. How can you insure that you too are passing on an inheritance of love to those who will come after you? In what way is your love sacrificial, though perhaps not in the extreme form of Harry's mother. Where is "the cross" in it?

HYMN: "O Love That Wilt Not Let me Go" or "Break Thou the Bread of Life"

A Prayer

Gracious God, whom we know as "Love," we thank you for talented writers and filmmakers who, whether they are conscious of it or not, serve you by declaring that truth, beauty, and love are what make life worth living. We are glad that millions of readers, young and old, find in the Harry Potter series meaning and inspiration, as well as entertainment. May your Spirit, which inspired those who wrote down in Holy Scripture the stories of your mighty acts, continue to inspire writers, filmmakers, and other artists. Even today may that same Spirit lead us to open our eyes, hearts, and minds to the truth contained in manifold works "beyond the sacred page." We ask this in the name of the One who is declared the Word, even Jesus Christ, our Lord. Amen.

19. *The Horse Whisperer*
Like the Patience of God

Bless the LORD, O my soul,
 and all that is within me,
 bless his holy name.
Bless the LORD, O my soul,
 and do not forget all his benefits—
who forgives all your iniquity,
 who heals all your diseases,
who redeems your life from the Pit,
 who crowns you with steadfast love and mercy,
who satisfies you with good as long as you live
 so that your youth is renewed like the eagle's.

The LORD works vindication
 and justice for all who are oppressed.
He made known his ways to Moses,
 his acts to the people of Israel.
The LORD is merciful and gracious,
 slow to anger and abounding in steadfast love.

Psalm 103:1–8

Love is patient; love is kind.

1 Corinthians 13:4

The fruit of the Spirit is love, joy, peace,
 patience. . . .

Galatians 5:22

Introduction

Tom Booker is a Montana cowboy respected by his peers as a "horse whisperer"—that rare human able to connect with horses in an almost mystical, understanding, and patient way. When veterinarians and their scientific methods and medicines are unable to help a distressed horse, their owners turn to a horse whisperer, often with wondrous results. New Yorker Annie MacLean reads about horse whisperers in a magazine article. She is a mother who is very involved in her career as a magazine editor and extremely worried about her daughter Grace and the girl's horse Pilgrim. Grace was involved in a terrible accident while out riding with her best friend. The friend was killed; Grace lost a leg; and Pilgrim's neck and face were terribly disfigured.

The internal scars are far worse than the physical ones for both girl and horse. Grace had resented her career-preoccupied mother anyway for the years of neglect. The trauma of the accident and its aftermath has just added to the distance between them. Annie, sensing that Grace's future well-being is tied in with Pilgrim's, resists the pleas of their vet to put the horse down. One cannot blame the veterinarian. The traumatized horse has become so unruly that no one can come near him without the risk of being kicked and trampled. The psychically damaged horse will not tolerate even Grace, who is herself so dispirited that she could not be of much help anyway. Annie, inspired by the magazine article, decides to contact Tom Booker by telephone. He tells her he is too busy and turns down her offer to fly him to New York to look at Pilgrim. Annie, refusing to take "No" for an answer, packs up her car, loads Pilgrim into a trailer, and, with Grace fussing and pouting beside her, sets off for Montana.

Tom Booker is surprised to see the three show up on the ranch he operates with his brother and sister-in-law. Annie refuses to be discouraged by his reluctance to become involved. Her persistence wins out. Tom tells her that he must know as much as possible about Pilgrim and Grace if he is to be able to help. He pins down the peevish Grace and gets her to agree to participate in the process by telling her that, without her cooperation, there is nothing he can do for Pilgrim. Although still resentful of her mother and of being dragged across the country to the ranch, Grace still loves the injured horse. She nods her assent. Over the next few days Tom does little with Pilgrim other than to be around him and allow him to settle into the new environment. Annie becomes acquainted with the family, and the two visitors are invited to eat with them at the ranch, and then, as they become better acquainted, to move from their motel to a vacant cabin. Annie, unused to the slow pace of ranch life, keeps in close connection with her New York office by cell phone, a device that she keeps constantly by her side.

The Scene

Time into film: 0:55:28   Stop at 1:02:35

It is early morning, and we see a quick shot of a church. Tom enters the corral and approaches Pilgrim. Successful in getting a halter on the horse, he and the ranch hands lead Pilgrim into a pool for bathing. All is going well, with Annie and Grace looking on. Then the ring of Annie's cell phone breaks the quietness. The skittish horse is spooked, rises up on its hind legs, knocks Tom into the water, and breaks away, dashing across a large meadow. Tom's nephew, rope in hand, starts to run after the horse, but Tom tells him to let it go. He then slowly walks toward the meadow, stopping at the edge, and hunches down. Pilgrim, feeding on the tall grass, stays on the far side.

The others watch a while, and Annie asks if there is

anything she can do. Tom ignores her. Tom's nephew and Grace watch, and exchange a few words; then the nephew goes off to do his chores. Annie asks if they should leave. Again no reply, so she does leave. Tom just sits and watches the horse. Time passes. Pilgrim continues to move about the meadow while eating, casting frequent glances back at Tom. He makes no move to approach the horse or even to call it. He just sits and waits. As the day progresses, we see Pilgrim feeding closer to Tom. Late afternoon arrives, and then early evening. The horse approaches and allows Tom to stretch out his hand to it. The horse whisperer pats and caresses Pilgrim gently. Together they walk back toward the distant barn. The accompanying music imparts a spiritual feeling to the scene. Annie has returned and witnesses the amazing rapprochement. Tom tells her not to bring the cell phone with her again.

Reflection on the Scene

When I first saw the film, this was the scene that most impressed me. It still does. Tom seemed like Yahweh in Psalm 103 dealing patiently with rebellious Israel. This is not the vengeful, wrathful Jehovah that so many associate with the Hebrew Scriptures, but the nurturing God "who forgives all your iniquity, who heals all your diseases." On the side of "the oppressed," the psalmist declares, "the LORD is merciful and gracious, slow to anger and abounding in steadfast love." Other Scripture writers agreed with the psalmist—indeed the phrase "steadfast love, and slow to anger" must have been like a proverb or saying, so often is it found in various combinations—in Exodus, Nehemiah, Joel, Jonah, and even Nahum. Time after time Israel goes astray, and time after time God calls the nation back.

Jesus also shows the patience of God in his parable of the Father and Two Sons. The father puts up with the outrageous request of the younger son. He patiently waits day after day for the boy to come to his senses and return home. His patience ends only when he catches sight of the young man trudging toward the family house, and then instead of standing on his dignity and waiting for the son to come near, the father runs out to him. Such patience, of course, is grounded in love. God's love for the nation he has created and that has rebelled against him is like that of this father's love for his wayward boy.

Tom's patience with Pilgrim is also based on love. A horse whisperer loves horses, feels something of what they feel, and wishes only the best for them. Most people seek a master-slave relationship with animals. They talk about "breaking" a colt so that it can be ridden. Some use whips and sharp spurs to goad a horse to faster speeds or to obey commands, and a harsh tone of voice to show who is in control. A horse whisperer takes a more nurturing approach, seeking a closer relationship. It is similar to what Martin Buber called an "I-thou" relationship, rather than an "I-it," for respect is given to the horse's nature and temperament. Thus this film scene can be seen as a visual parable, reminding us of something important about God—and also how we should relate to one another. The nurturing, feminine side of God is being reclaimed, as it needs to be. This film can be used to help us see that side.

The view of a wrathful God ready to strike down sinners is still very much with us. It has some truth, in that God is concerned with righteousness, and there is a penalty to be paid for sin. God's wrath is held in tension in the Bible with God's mercy, divine justice accompanied by love. There can be no separating them, but neither can be given up. And it is the merciful and slow-to-anger side that we especially need to emulate. The author of the book of Proverbs recognized this (see 14:29 and 16:32), as did the New Testament writers James (1:19) and Paul, the latter seeing patience as a "fruit of the Spirit." God's wrath was always seen as having a purpose, when sinners either repented, or in hard cases, when they were destroyed. But "the mercy of the Lord endures forever."

For Further Reflection

1. If Tom had chased Pilgrim, thrown him to the ground and tethered him, what would have been the result? Dominance, perhaps—but cooperation? (See the delightful *Babe*, a film in which domination versus cooperation is a main theme.) And ultimately, healing? How is cooperation from the afflicted important if healing is to take place?

2. How in the rest of the film does Tom's approach help the tormented Grace? Her mother? Notice how Tom had to pull back from his own feelings for and relationship with the married Annie in order for the latter to deal with her own troubles, both with Grace and with her husband.

3. Has the angry God, impatient with sin and sinners, been a part of your religious upbringing? How have you reconciled this with the God of "mercy and loving-kindness"?

4. What are some events in your life in which you can now see that God has dealt patiently with you? How does believing in this kind of Creator make it easier to approach God?

5. Are there languishing relationships in your life that need a measure of loving patience?

HYMN: "Praise, My Soul, the King of Heaven" (especially vv. 2 and 3)

A Prayer

Merciful and gracious God, slow to anger and abounding in steadfast love, we thank you for the many ways in which you have patiently dealt with us through the years. Even when we have been impatient and demanding, you have treated us with the tender care of a mother. As we all too slowly grow in awareness of your nature and the path you would have us follow, help us to share with others the good news of your immeasurable, patient love. Help us to seek to cooperate with, not to dominate, those whom you send as companions, that together we might discover the dignity you place in each of us. Amen.

20. *In the Bedroom*
When Grief Blocks Forgiveness

How could we sing the LORD's song
    in a foreign land?
If I forget you, O Jerusalem,
    let my right hand wither!
Let my tongue cling to the roof of my mouth,
    if I do not remember you,
if I do not set Jerusalem
    above my highest joy.
Remember, O LORD, against the Edomites
    the day of Jerusalem's fall,
how they said, "Tear it down! Tear it down!

Down to its foundations!"
O daughter Babylon, you devastator!
   Happy shall they be who pay you back
   what you have done to us!
Happy shall they be who take your little ones
and dash them against the rock!

Psalm 137:4–9

Then Peter came and said to him, "Lord, if another member of the church sins against me, how often should I forgive? As many as seven times?" Jesus said to him, "Not seven times, but, I tell you, seventy-seven times."

Matthew 18:21–22

Beloved, never avenge yourselves, but leave room for the wrath of God; for it is written, "Vengeance is mine, I will repay, says the Lord." No, "if your enemies are hungry, feed them; if they are thirsty, give them something to drink; for by doing this you will heap burning coals on their heads." Do not be overcome by evil, but overcome evil with good.

Romans 12:19–21

Introduction

Not since Atom Egoyan's *The Sweet Hereafter* has raw grief and its potential for poisoning the human soul been depicted so well on the screen. As the film begins we meet Matt and Ruth Fowler, a happy couple living in a small, coastal Maine town. They seem to have an idyllic life, living in a comfortable house in a postcard-perfect village. However, they are worried about the relationship of their college-age son Nick with

Natalie Strout. Not only is she older than Nick, but also she has children and is still married to an abusive husband, Richard. The two are separated, but the jealous Richard is not willing to face reality and admit that his marriage is over. Ruth asks Matt to do something about the situation, but her passive husband tells her that things will work out. Things do, but in a horribly different way than even Ruth had feared—the volatile Richard kills Nick. Richard comes over to Natalie's home and starts to hit her. Nick is there and rushes in to defend her. In his rage Richard kills the one whom he views as a threat to his plans to reunite with his wife.

The Fowlers have to live with their guilt and grief. To make matters worse, Richard is set free until the trial. Because of Richard's ties with the community, the judge does not set the usual high bail. It is such a small town that Ruth cannot avoid seeing him at times. She and Matt retreat into their grief and barely talk. They meet with the public prosecutor, who warns them that the upcoming trial will be a difficult ordeal. It is even possible that Richard will be found not guilty. He is claiming self-defense, and his lawyer will paint the dead Nick as a home wrecker. Thus each sighting of Richard about town seems to the parents like a nail driven into their skin.

The Scene

Time into film: 1:24:50   Stop at 1:37:35

Ruth is sitting at a table in the school auditorium. A music teacher, she is listening to a recording when Natalie enters the hall and slowly approaches the table. "I want to talk," she hesitantly says to Ruth. She then asks for forgiveness. Ruth takes off the headphones and rises. Suddenly, without a word, she slaps Natalie hard on her cheek. The girl is stunned. Staring at her assailant for a moment, she then turns and walks up the aisle and leaves the hall. Ruth calmly puts the earphones back on and resumes listening to the tape.

On her way home Ruth stops at the store to buy a bag of groceries. At the counter the clerk stares past her, and Ruth turns to see who it is. It is Richard. Nodding to the clerk to indicate he has poured a drink into the cup he is holding, he quickly leaves the store. Ruth is visibly upset but stays in control. Not for long, though.

Back in her own kitchen she is unpacking the groceries when Matt comes in. To his "How are things going?" she frostily replies, "Fine." He knows better, so he presses her. "Something wrong?" "Wrong? What could be wrong?" She finally relates her encounter with their son's killer at the store. Matt says they should talk about things, and she sarcastically answers, "We haven't before! Why should we now?" Thus begins a battle royal between the two, each grieving in such different ways.

Ruth accuses Matt of not having any feelings, and then implies that Matt is to blame for their son's death. This charge infuriates him. He tries to defend himself, but Ruth is angry that he did nothing to break up the romance of the couple that she believed from the start were wrong for each other. Matt says that he thought things would work out. Oh yes, they did, Ruth accuses him—they worked out in the death of their son. She agonizingly says that she misses him, even if Matt doesn't seem to. As they tear at each other, Matt drops his bombshell, accusing Ruth of always being controlling. He goes back years to a Little League game when she yanked Nick out of the game for a reason important only to her. He tells her that everything their son did seemed to be wrong in her eyes. "Well, what *was* wrong with him?" he asks. "You are so unforgiving!" he charges, and adds, "That's what he said. And you're pulling that same sh - - with me!" This leaves Ruth devastated.

The doorbell interrupts them. Matt goes to discover that their callers are a couple of girls selling candy for a school benefit. He buys several bars and brings them back to Ruth. Apparently thinking during this interval about what he has just said, he tells his wife, "I'm sorry. I had no right." She admits that he had been right about the unforgiving, relating for him what she had done to Natalie just a short time ago. The two talk some more, embracing and speaking about the future. It becomes evident that Matt is not going to be so passive any more, but as we shall see as the rest of the movie unfolds, it will not be an improvement in his character or their situation.

Reflection on the Scene

The Fowlers seem to lack the resources of a warm, vital faith to find any consolation in their situation. For them their forced separation from their only son is forever, and they cannot bear it. Like the writer of Psalm 137, who was uprooted from his home and marched off to Babylon when Judah was defeated, Ruth and Matt have entered the "foreign land" of sorrow. Thus the hatred that would gladly dash against rocks the babies of the enemy spreads unchecked through their hearts and minds. Any thought of forgiving is blocked by their bitter grief and anger. Matt loves his wife and cannot stand to see her so convulsed—especially as the trial progresses and it appears that Richard might actually be freed to haunt them in the village for the rest of their lives. Aroused from his passive state, he concocts a plan that will add to the horror of the death of their son by bringing about a rough form of justice.

We want the film to end in the usual Hollywood way, wherein all is forgiven and reconciliation transforms the characters, but things are not always resolved in life in such a manner. The Fowlers are decent people, but they too can become capable of terrible things. If even the writer of one of the most sublime of the Psalms, the 139th, could write, "O that you would kill the wicked, O God, and that the bloodthirsty would depart from me—" (v. 19) and, "I hate them with perfect hatred; I count them my enemies," (v. 22), it should not surprise us what the grieving father does. The psalmist is honest enough to express the rage tearing at his heart. There is no hiding behind sweet pious words here. Hatred is something we all have probably felt at one time or another. Fortunately for most of us, the feeling passes, sooner if there is a faith based on love to displace it. The third stanza of Rosamond E. Herklots's hymn "Forgive Our Sins as We Forgive" offers us much wisdom:

"How can Your pardon reach and bless The unforgiving heart

That broods on wrongs and will not let Old bitterness depart?"*

Such is the case with Ruth and Matt. The hymnwriter could be addressing them. Probably only those who have actually lost a child to murder can really know or understand what the Fowlers are going through.

---

* Hymn no. 347 in *The Presbyterian Hymnal* (Louisville, Ky.: Westminster/John Knox Press, 1990.) Text © Oxford University Press.

This searing film might be as close to our knowing as is possible. *In the Bedroom* is a difficult film to watch. As a parable of the effect of unrelieved sorrow and anger that blocks forgiveness, it is unforgettable.

For Further Reflection

1. What times of sorrow have you known? How was the sorrow relieved? If a death, how did the rites of the church help? How did friends and fellow church members help?

2. How do the feelings of guilt and anger complicate sorrow?

3. What grudges have you or someone you know held against those who have wronged you? Have you been able to overcome them, and if so, how? What can happen when a person is not able to let go of anger and hatred?

4. What do you think of the stories of parents able to forgive the killers of their children or family members? What must they have had to do to be able to forgive?

5. For true stories of people who have been able to "move on" with their lives by forgiving, see the two videos *Journey Toward Forgiveness* and *Killing Time: The Noel Fellowes Story*. If your local library or church resource center does not have them, both are available from Vision Video, P.O. Box 540, Worcester, PA 19490, or infor@visionvideo.com, or 1-800-523-0226.

HYMN: "Forgive Our Sins as We Forgive"

A Prayer

O God, we pray for all those who sorrow, especially for those who have lost a loved one killed by someone else, whether by intention or accident. Fill them with your comfort and the knowledge that you as a parent gave up your Son to be murdered by angry people. Remove bitterness, reckless rage, and let love drive out hatred, that healing can begin and brokenness be replaced by wholeness. May we own up to hatred and other forms of darkness within us, arising from the hurts that we receive, to the end that we might place them before you, entrusting all that we are, the bad and the good, to your care. We ask this in the name of the One, who even while wracked with pain and taunts during his long dying hours, called out to you, "Father, forgive them, for they do not know what they do." Amen.

21. *The Iron Giant*
Humans and Machines—
Little Lower than Angels?

I call heaven and earth to witness against you today that I have set before you life and death, blessings and curses. Choose life so that you and your descendants may live . . .

Deuteronomy 30:19–20

For everything there is a season, and a time for
        every matter under heaven:
    a time to be born, and a time to die;
    a time to plant, and a time to pluck up what is
        planted;

. . . .

For the fate of humans and the fate of animals is the same; as one dies, so dies the other. They all have the same breath, and humans have no advantage over the animals; for all is vanity. All go to one place; all are from the dust, and all turn to dust again. Who knows whether the human spirit goes upward and the spirit of animals goes downward to the earth?

Ecclesiastes 3:1–2, 19–21

When I look at your heavens, the work of your
   fingers,
   the moon and the stars that you have
   established;
What are human beings that you are mindful of
   them,
   mortals that you care for them?

Psalm 8:3–4

I believe that man will not merely endure; he will prevail. He is immortal, not because he alone among creatures has an inexhaustible voice, but because he has a soul, a spirit capable of compassion and sacrifice and endurance.

William Faulkner: Nobel Prize acceptance
speech, 1950

Introduction

Brad Bird, a creative consultant to and occasional director of the hit television series *The Simpsons*, has given us a wonderful adaptation of British poet Ted Hughes's children's book, known in the United Kingdom as *The Iron Man*. With the latter author's blessing he has given the original story an American spin, setting it in the small town of Rockwell, Maine, during the height of the Cold War. Sputnik has been launched. Rock and roll is on the rise. The Russians have the atomic bomb. Berlin has been under siege. Spies and traitors, so it was believed, are everywhere. Children at school are led through drills to prepare

them for an atomic blast. The Cold War antagonism
and paranoia are reflected in the media, especially the
films depicting ruthless aliens from outer space invading earth.

The story of the boy Hogarth is set against the above
background, so when he encounters in the woods a 50-
foot robot, he is terrified. But when the boy discovers
that the robot is a kindly giant, more like a curious child
than a monster, able to talk by mimicking Hogarth's
words, he decides to hide his new friend. Realizing the
terror that such a creature would cause among the fearful citizens of his village, Hogarth does not even tell his
single-parent mom, Annie. Eventually he does enlist his
grown-up friend Dean in hiding the Iron Giant in the
junkyard, which Dean runs as part of his vocation of a
metal sculpture artist. The Iron Giant has a voracious
appetite for metal, so what better place to conceal him?
The apprehensive Dean would like to come up with
several alternatives, but he agrees that Hogarth's plan is
for the best.

It is not easy keeping the presence of a 50-foot robot
a secret, so there are some funny scenes of Hogarth
trying to keep the Iron Giant under cover. Rumors
start flying around the village about a mysterious creature wandering in the woods. Soon Washington has
dispatched the arrogant, suspicious agent Kent
Mansley to investigate. Hogarth takes an immediate
dislike to Mansley, sensing that he is both devious and
prone to shoot first and ask questions later. Matters
escalate until the military is called out. In their pursuit
of the Iron Giant they threaten to destroy the whole
town, with Hogarth frantically trying to intervene and
get them to listen to reason. It is only through a great
sacrifice that annihilation of the town is finally prevented.

If you liked *The Day the Earth Stood Still* and *ET,* the two films it somewhat resembles, you should enjoy *The Iron Giant.* This film succeeds well as wholesome family entertainment, with some of its humor and references to the '50s aimed at adults, and its message of love and acceptance directed at all ages.

The Scene

Time into film: 0:50:28   Stop at 0:52:51

Hogarth and the Iron Giant are out in the woods when they encounter a beautiful deer. The giant bends down to touch it gently, but it runs off. Moments later they hear a shot. The Iron Giant is as taken aback as is Hogarth when they come upon hunters who have shot the graceful creature. When they see the robot, the hunters yell, "It's a monster!" and run away. As they look at the lifeless deer, the giant starts to pick up the lifeless body. Fearful that his friend's huge hand will squeeze it, Hogarth commands him to stop, "Don't do that!" Hogarth tells his friend that the deer is dead, killed by the gun. "Gun?" the robot repeats, looking at the weapon that the hunters had dropped in their hasty exit. The eyes of the robot seem to focus on the dropped object as they turn red with what we assume is anger. "What's wrong?" the boy asks worriedly. "Guns kill," the boy says, and the Iron Giant repeats the phrase. "It's bad to kill," the boy states, "but it's not bad to die."

That night, back in the junkyard, Hogarth continues their conversation. He tells his friend that he knows that he feels bad about the deer, but things die. "It's a part of life." "You die?" the curious robot asks. "Yes, someday." "I die?" asks the robot. Hogarth, now deep in thought, muses, "You're made of metal, but you have feelings, and you think about things—and that means you have a soul. And souls don't die." "Soul?" his friend asks. "Mom says it's something inside all good things, and that it goes on forever and ever," answers Hogarth. The big creature turns over with the sound of metal scraping against grass and soil and looks up at the stars. Contemplating this big idea he repeats, "Souls don't die."

Reflection on the Scene

Little wonder that adults enjoy this film as much as children. It explores some big ideas in its own way just as deeply as such films as *Blade Runner, A.I.: Artificial Intelligence, Bicentennial Man,* and *Star Trek: Generations.* Hogarth and his mother are not depicted as church-goers, but they apparently are interested in things of the spirit and have talked together about them. What a wonderful opportunity this film offers, and this scene in particular, for parents, pastors, and church-school teachers to talk with children about deep matters. Hogarth probably has never read William Faulkner's Nobel Awards acceptance speech, but his childlike wisdom leads him to leap to a similar conclusion as did the great author. The boy sees in his metallic friend "a spirit capable of compassion and sacrifice and endurance," and so he concludes that the Iron Giant has a soul.

Although Hogarth's belief that the soul is indestructible might be more akin to Greek philosophy than to Hebrew-Christian thought (which posits "resurrection," rather than immortality of a soul), the scene is a rare moment in an animated film, one in which a character recognizes that we are spiritual as well as material beings—and in which it is suggested that even a machine, if it possess curiosity, good will, and a conscience, as the Iron Giant apparently does, is more than just a machine. Later, when the Iron Giant is about to use the terrible weapons built into him to wreak havoc upon their enemies, Hogarth pleads with his friend, telling him, "You don't have to be a gun. You choose what you want to be." That moment is equivalent to the one when Joshua urged his people, "Choose life so that you and your descendants may live."

I suspect that were the psalmist to encounter the Iron Giant, he might have asked the same question raised deep within him by his contemplation of the starry heavens: "What are human beings that you are mindful of them, mortals that you care for them?" As our technology-based culture grows, producing computers that "think," the line dividing humans and machines is going to become more and more elusive and puzzling. It's good now to take time out, after enjoying the story of *The Iron Giant*, to reflect about and discuss the big ideas that it raises, even with, or maybe, *especially* with, our children.

Thus far we have thought about machines raised to the level of humans, but there are also some philosophies and political ideologies that would reduce humans to machines. Certainly the Nazis and the Communists, the latter in practice if not in theory, saw individual humans as interchangeable and expendable. They were to serve the state. This seems to be the case with those today who see the public as consumers, existing to keep the economy going by buying, using, and disposing an endless supply of things. The last thing advertisers want their targets to do is to lie under the stars at night and reflect on such subjects as "death and killing" and "soul," or realize that they can resist manipulation and, as Hogarth and the Iron Giant do, freely make a choice.

For Further Reflection

1. Who, or what, are we? Where have we come from, and where do you believe we are going?

2. What do you believe about death? Do you believe that there is anything beyond this life? What does your church teach about this? What do other faiths teach?

3. How close is the dividing line between machines and animals? Those who have seen *Blade Runner, A.I.: Artificial Intelligence, Bicentennial Man*, and *Star Trek: Generations*—what answers do these films suggest? Some are fearful that by our science we will take the place of God: what do you think about this? Can we place limits on our scientific ventures? Should we? What happened when the church tried this with Galileo and other such explorers of the unknown?

4. Do you feel at times that you or other people have been reduced to a machine? What is the difference between humans and machines?

HYMN: "God, Who Stretched the Spangled Heavens" or "I Sing the Mighty Power of God"

A Prayer

Gracious God, our Creator, in your Word you declare that you have fashioned us in your image. Thus we too are born to create, but as our creations, and the society which they shape, grow ever more complex and amazing, we are threatened by arrogance and confusion and fear. Arrogance because we sometimes think that we are on a par with you, no longer in need of your guidance and grace. Confusion because we see the blurring of the lines that once so clearly divided us from you, the animals, and the machines that we have made. And fear because we are so uncertain of where all this is leading us. By your Spirit help us to think about the big questions and the mysteries of our lives, that we will not fear the future nor ever feel that we have moved beyond your caring presence and love. We ask this in the name of Jesus Christ, the pioneer of our faith. Amen.

22. *It's a Wonderful Life*
"The Richest Man in Town"

> Now there was a great outcry of the people and of their wives against their Jewish kin. For there were those who said, "With our sons and our daughters, we are many; we must get grain, so that we may eat and stay alive." There were also those who said, "We are having to pledge our fields, our vineyards, and our houses in order to get grain during the famine." And there were those who said, "We are having to borrow money on our fields and vineyards to pay the king's tax. Now our flesh is the same as that of our kindred; our children are the same as their children; and yet we are forcing our sons and daughters to be slaves, and some of our daughters have been ravished; we are powerless, and our fields and vineyards now belong to others."
>
> I was very angry when I heard their outcry and these complaints. After thinking it over, I brought charges against the nobles and the officials; I said to them, "You are all taking interest from your own people."
>
> Nehemiah 5:1–7

The perverse get what their ways deserve,
and the good, what their deeds deserve.

Proverbs 14:14

"Do not store up for yourselves treasures on earth, where moth and rust consume and where thieves break in and steal; but store up for yourselves treasures in heaven, where neither moth nor rust consumes and where thieves do not break in and steal. For where your treasure is, there your heart will be also."

Matthew 6:19–21

Introduction

Is there a person in the United States or Canada who does not know the story of George Bailey and the despair that almost results in his taking his own life during the Christmas season? Of how his attempts to help his fellow citizens of Bedford Falls seemed to be ending in failure as his archenemy, the greedy Mr. Potter, was just about to succeed in destroying the bank founded by George's father? And how the novice angel Clarence won his wings by preventing George from committing suicide by showing him how dreadful the town would have been if he had never been born? (In case you are that rare person, you can catch the film on about any channel during December—or borrow or rent it from your video store or public library!)

In his confrontation with Potter, who wants to totally dominate Bedford Falls, George is very much like Nehemiah, who confronted the leaders of his day who were oppressing their own people. I believe that the author of Proverbs would have liked this film, in which Potter gets what he deserves—the disdain of the people of Bedford Falls. And George receives his reward, the love and support of the many people whom he has helped along the way, indicating that he has indeed, by his years of self-sacrifice, laid up for himself "treasures in heaven." But before this happens the grasping Mr. Potter finds the bag that Uncle Billy had misplaced with its $8,000 of the bank's money. Knowing that the loss of this money would ruin George's bank, Potter spreads the rumor that George's bank is failing because of missing money. This misinformation creates a panic with hundreds of depositors rushing to take out their money, leaving George broke and so dispirited that he contemplates suicide. And then comes his momentous encounter with the angel Clarence and his learning what life in Bedford Falls would have been like had he never lived. Quite a bleak place! This gives George a new outlook and a strong desire to go back home and face the consequences, come what may.

The Scene

Time into film: 2:02:50   Stop at 2:09:50 ("The End")

After George discovers that he is back in Bedford Falls and his hasty wish not to have been born is cancelled, he is overjoyed, hugging the policeman and fairly shouting his joy. He even stops before the window of Potter's office to wish him "Merry Christmas." He cavorts through the streets and arrives home to find the bank examiner and a bevy of reporters to record his arrest. George gives them a friendly greeting, seemingly glad about the missing $8,000 and the prospect of going to jail, so happy is he to be alive again. He dashes upstairs and hugs his children. He asks where is Mary, and they answer that she has gone out.

Soon Mary rushes back in, her anxiety melting as she sees her husband back safe and sound. She leads him down the stairway and plants him beside the family Christmas tree in the living room, excitedly saying, "George, it's a miracle!" Uncle Billy comes in with a crowd of people, all beaming and greeting George. A basket-full of money is dumped out before him. Others bring their own contributions, some in purses, one in a big jar. A man even gives George his watch. The woman who had transferred her account to Potter's safer bank is back. They tell George that when they heard of his predicament, they had to come. One man tells him that he wouldn't have had a roof over his head if weren't for George. A telegram is brought in from George's high school chum pledging $25,000 to get the bank back on its feet. George stares, overcome with emotion. And then his brother arrives, having just flown in to the airport. There is still snow on his aviator's hat. It is he who gives the memorable toast that sums up George's life, "To my brother, the richest man in town." George receives a book. It is a copy of *Tom Sawyer*, with a note inside that reads, "No man is a failure when he has friends." It is signed, "Clarence."

Reflection on the Scene

George is indeed "the richest man in town," though not in any way that his archenemy Potter could understand. He will never own a fancy car or house or have a huge bank account, for he is too concerned with the welfare of his neighbors to accumulate the things that Potter treasures. But George is surrounded by people who admire and love him. Potter is alone, with only hired flunkies to keep him company. He is rich in things but poor in matters of the spirit.

We do not know whether George goes to church or not, but if he does, the hymn "Be Thou My Vision," based on an old Irish poem, could be one of his favorites, especially the second verse:

> Riches I heed not nor vain, empty praise,
> Thou mine inheritance, now and always:
> Thou and Thou only first in my heart,
> Great God of heaven, my treasure Thou art.
> (No. 339, *The Presbyterian Hymnal*)

Frank Capra's film is as schmaltzy as they come, but it has endured for half a century because it affirms some basic values, values that we know are absolutely necessary if we are to have a livable society. Without being overtly Christian, the film celebrates the values taught by Jesus—compassion and concern for others; courage in opposing evil; resolution in withstanding temptation; love strong enough to carry a cross. Each Christmas the film continues to remind its advertisement-saturated audiences what is important in life, and helps keep alive the hope that we can do a little better during the next year.

For Further Reflection

1. Have you felt left behind at times, like George, when you see others who are able to afford many more things than you have?

2. What values are affirmed in the film? Borrow the plot device and imagine: what would your town be like without these values? Who would lose, and who would benefit? What would happen to the churches and other people-serving organizations and agencies? Would you want to live in such a place?

3. What "treasures" do you think you have you laid up that will grow over the years, enriching your relationship with God and your family and friends? How rich are you in friends? In your spiritual life? How have your friends enriched or supported you at crucial moments in your life?

HYMN: "Be Thou My Vision"

A Prayer

Gracious God, we thank you for calling the George Baileys of this world to do your works of compassion and mercy. Grant that neither they nor we will give way to discouragement when others oppose or misunderstand those works. Strengthen us in your Spirit that we might lay up for ourselves treasures in heaven by doing your will here on earth. In Christ's name we pray. Amen.

23. *Italian for Beginners*
A Faith That Listens and Challenges

Then the LORD answered Job out of the whirlwind:
"Who is this that darkens counsel by words without knowledge?"

Job 38:1–2

The LORD is my chosen portion and my cup;
    you hold my lot.
The boundary lines have fallen for me in pleasant places;
    I have a goodly heritage.

I bless the LORD who gives me counsel;
   in the night also my heart instructs me.
I keep the LORD always before me;
      because he is at my right hand, I shall not be
         moved.

Therefore my heart is glad, and my soul rejoices;
   my body also rests secure.
For you do not give me up to Sheol,
   or let your faithful one see the Pit.

You show me the path of life.
   In your presence there is fullness of joy;
   in your right hand are pleasures forevermore.
                                                      Psalm 16:5–11

As God's chosen ones, holy and beloved, clothe
yourselves with compassion, kindness, humility,
meekness, and patience. Bear with one another
and, if anyone has a complaint against another,
forgive each other; just as the Lord has forgiven
you, so you also must forgive. Above all, clothe
yourselves with love, which binds everything
together in perfect harmony.
                                                      Colossians 3:12-14

Introduction

In this romantic film we follow the paths of six
Copenhagen suburbanites. Some are grieving, but all
are lonely and desperately looking to connect with
others. They work at and live near a suburban complex
that houses a sports facility, a hotel and restaurant, a
hair salon, and a church close by. It will be a night
school class of conversational Italian that will draw

them all into each other's worlds, melding them together into one in the delightful climax when the whole class travels to Italy at last.

Andreas is the central character, relating in different ways to all the others. A young pastor, he has come to replace the former, demented, pastor of the church. Besides vociferously berating his parishioners, Rev. Wredmann, the former pastor, has refused to vacate the vicarage, so Andreas is directed to the hotel, where the desk manager Jorgen Mortensen befriends him. The hostile antics of Wredmann have emptied the church of most of its worshipers, so that on one occasion the communion service is cancelled because there are only two women in attendance, besides the two wardens and the pastor. Wredmann's heckling of the new pastor from the balcony does not help matters, and for a long time there is no organist, even for funerals. Andreas is told that he is in the hospital. A little later we learn that Wredmann was responsible for this. During an argument over the proper tempo for a hymn he became so enraged that he shoved the organist off the balcony. In the scene that we will look at, we discover that the two pastors are alike in one respect. Each has lost a wife—but each responds very differently to his wife's death.

Former athlete Jorgen Mortensen helps orient Andreas to his new surroundings, suggesting that one way to fill his lonely nights would be to join the class in Italian. Andreas seems so open and accepting that Jorgen soon is confiding in him, even seeking advice about how to overcome his impotence. This is of special concern because he is drawn to the lovely Guilia, the cook working in the hotel restaurant. She does not speak Danish, so Jorgen's desire to communicate with her motivates him to attend the newly formed class.

The hotel restaurant presents Jorgen with a problem. It is presided over by Hal-Finn, a no-nonsense crusty manager who berates any customers whom he thinks lack table manners or who dare to complain about the food. The owner tells Jorgen to fire Hal-Finn, but the kindhearted man cannot bring himself to do so. He does tell the shaggy-haired Finn to get a haircut, but that is about as far as he can go. The problem solves itself later during a terrible fracas between Finn and a customer. When Finn does go for a haircut, he is immediately attracted to Karen, a woman who has such problems caring for her dying mother that each time Finn shows up for the haircut, the telephone rings, summoning her to come and deal with an emergency.

Karen's mother has not been an easy person to care for, always criticizing and complaining to her daughter. But now in the hospital she is a most pitiable case, requiring more and more morphine to keep the intense pain at bay. Karen and another member of the Italian class both find in Andreas a compassionate counselor. The other woman is Olympia, also caring for a parent near the end of his days. Her thankless father also constantly scolds and complains. Olympia, who becomes romantically drawn to the pastor, works at a bakery, where she is constantly dropping trays of goods. She confesses to Andreas that she has held forty-three jobs, her clumsiness leading to dismissal each time. She has been able to hold onto her current position only because she pays for the spoiled goods out of her own salary. At first her clumsiness seems like a touch of comedy, something to lighten up things, but when we learn the cause of it, our hearts reach out to this barely coping woman.

The Italian class is threatened with cancellation when their teacher suddenly drops dead. Fortunately Hal-Finn

is proficient in the language because he once hung out
with an Italian soccer team. He agrees to take over as
teacher, which actually is a good thing, because he has
just lost his job at the restaurant. With Andreas now
enrolling, it looks as if the class will not be cancelled.
Thus is he thrust into the middle of their hopes, dreams,
and their problems, some trivial, some heartbreaking.

The Scene

Warning: Although there are no objectionable elements in the scene on which this meditation is based,
the film is R-rated because of sexual content and some
vulgar expletives uttered by a couple of the characters.
If you show the entire film to a group, be sure to warn
of the two love scenes. There is no nudity, but the passionate grappling of the two characters leaves little to
the imagination.

Time into film: 1:10:27   Stop at 1:14:58

Apparently wanting a showdown with Pastor
Wredmann, Andreas rings his doorbell one evening.
He wishes Wredmann "Merry Christmas," but the
man replies, "You don't know the meaning of
Christmas!" Wredmann seems confused at first, but
when Andreas asks whether he thinks he should accept
the offer to become the resident pastor—the
Christmas service had been packed with worshipers
appreciative of the young man's ministry—the older
man scornfully retorts that Andreas could not become
the shepherd of a large church. Finally getting
Wredmann to allow him to enter the house, the usually shy Andreas mounts an attack on the former pastor's cynical dismissal of God.

Andreas affirms that God does exist for those who
believe. Wredmann then opens up, revealing the

source of his current sad predicament. Stating that his wife has been dead for four years, he adds, "God took her away from me, and she took God away from me." He pours out his heart as he describes how her fatal illness seemed to make her slowly disappear. When Andreas tries to respond, Wredmann attacks him by saying that he does not know the meaning of loss. Whether the man does not know that Andreas is a widower or whether he just dismisses the knowledge is unclear. Probably the latter, because Andreas fires back, "That doesn't give you the right to run the church into the ground! Your grief is no different from anyone else's here!"

The full measure of Wredmann's arrogance is revealed by his response: "Elizabeth wasn't like the other meaningless people we have to keep burying!" Andreas brushes this aside, telling him to leave the people alone. "You have no idea what you are talking about!" the old man declares. "You don't know pain or loss or love!" No longer able to contain himself in the presence of such insensitivity, Andreas shouts, "I know what I'm talking about! You are so deeply, deeply selfish, Wredmann! Get on with your life!" No one probably ever has talked to the arrogant Wredmann in such a way before. He shuts up, apparently left with no words of retort.

In the very next scene we see Andreas in a different situation. He is swimming in the hotel pool when Jorgen, troubled over his inability to approach Giulia, asks for some advice. Andreas suggests that he invite the girl for a walk. At the Italian class we hear Jorgen practicing the Italian for the invitation. At the end of class the usually self-confident Finn asks Andreas to stay for five minutes. His temper had caused a rift between himself and Karen. He wonders what he should do. The pastor suggests that he should say to her that he's sorry, but Finn replies that she is to blame. "In that case, begin by forgiving her," says Andreas.

Reflection on the Scene

The way the various stories of the quirky characters are interwoven is a delight, and especially the many times in which the pastor serves as an agent of grace. With the distraught Pastor Wredmann, grace takes the form of tough love, forcing the man to confront his self-centeredness. Hopefully he has been made to realize that he had been using his grief as an excuse for dropping out of life. Andreas seeks to push him back into it. Each of the other hurting characters also receives from Andreas just what she or he needs at the moment, helping the person to move ahead in their tangled affairs. For them grace often comes in the form of a listening ear and a word of encouragement or a simple, but timely word.

We never are shown any of the actual church services led by Andreas, nor do we hear any of his sermons. We can guess at the effectiveness of the latter, thanks to a brief scene in which Andreas is going over in his mind one of his homilies. He says that God is around and among us, present in an embrace or other act of love. Thus his theology is a very incarnational one. It is apparent that God is very much present in him as he informally tends to the needs of his friends. It is good to see such a positive image for a change of the church and one of its leaders. Andreas is human, needing companionship and love, and yet he is an effective counselor and leader (probably because of this). The once-empty church begins to fill up as, both in sermon and in his relationships with people, he offers a positive, hopeful gospel. This is one of those absorbing, uplifting little films for which we should thank God that there are filmmakers willing, even in a romantic comedy-drama, to tackle such matters of the spirit.

For Further Reflection

1. Does your pastor seem more like the confident but distant Pastor Wredmann or the warm, approachable shepherd not afraid to show his own vulnerability, like Andreas? (A difficult question, of course, if you, dear reader, are a pastor. But think back and ask how often over the years people have sought you out. Do you work behind a closed door, or is yours usually open so that people feel that they can drop by? Do children seem to be comfortable in your presence, and do they enjoy sharing a secret or question with you? How many of your people's homes have you been in during the past month—or do CEO matters keep you so busy that there is no time for shepherding?)

2. What do you think of Andreas's confrontation with Wredmann? How is tough love often what such a person needs? What is the proper role of sorrow and grief, and when do they become obstructive to faith?

3. What do you think of Wredmann's statement that God took his wife? Where or when have you heard this before? How does this blaming God make it easier to behave as Wredmann does? We are not shown how Andreas responded to his wife's death immediately after her passing, but how could we surmise that he did, based on what we see him say and do in the film? How do the two men demonstrate the difference between a me-centered and a God-centered faith?

4. How do you see the Scriptures quoted at the beginning incarnate in the life and acts of Andreas? In the lives of friends or loved ones? In your own faith and life?

Hymn: "I Need Thee Every Hour" or "Nearer My God to Thee"

A Prayer

Gracious and ever-present Creator, fill us with your Spirit that we might be aware that you are close by, even when our hearts are broken and tears stream down our cheeks. We know that your Son wept before a tomb, and that his body was placed in one also. Therefore we are able to believe that you know and understand our hearts when they are broken and cry out for relief. Help us to see that because of what we go through, we will be able to shepherd others through similar situations. We thank you for a film in which we are shown such a role model of caring. Even though he is the product of the creativity and skill of many artists—the writer and director, the actor, and the camera crew—may his memory linger long in our hearts and minds, enriching our faith and strengthening our resolve to reach out to others. In the name of the Good Shepherd we pray. Amen.

24. *Magnolia*
Prodigal Son, Prodigal Father

Turn to me and be gracious to me,
    for I am lonely and afflicted.
Relieve the troubles of my heart,
    and bring me out of my distress.
Consider my affliction and my trouble,
    and forgive all my sins.

Psalm 25:16-18

Then Jesus said, "There was a man who had two sons. . . . But when he came to himself he said, . . . 'But we had to celebrate and rejoice, because this brother of yours was dead and has come to life; he was lost and has been found.'"

From Luke 15:11–32

From now on, therefore, we regard no one from a human point of view; even though we once knew Christ from a human point of view, we know him no longer in that way. So if anyone is in Christ, there is a new creation: everything old has passed away; see, everything has become new! All this is from God, who reconciled us to himself through Christ, and has given us the ministry of reconciliation; that is, in Christ God was reconciling the world to himself, not counting their trespasses against them, and entrusting the message of reconciliation to us. So we are ambassadors for Christ, since God is making his appeal through us; we entreat you on behalf of Christ, be reconciled to God.

2 Corinthians 5:16–20

Introduction

Paul Thomas Anderson's *Magnolia* is a dark yet hopeful series of stories about people desperately trying to connect with one another. In fact it is difficult to keep up with the various stories and characters due to the frequent cutting back and forth between them. Each person in the film has just about given up on life, so overwhelming are his or her circumstances and failures. The story we concentrate on here presents us with a man at the terminal point of life. Earl Partridge has been a big success as a television producer, amassing a fortune but along the way losing his son, and maybe his soul. Earl has always found it difficult to be around suffering, and now he himself is dying a slow, painful death. Years before, when his son was a teenager, Earl's first wife, Lily, had contracted cancer. Unable to cope with the agony of watching someone he loved so much die, he had walked away from the family, leaving the son to nurse his mother—and his rage against his absent father. Earl also is wracked with guilt because he had been unfaithful to his wife so often, even during the years when she was in good health.

Earl's second wife, Linda, is much younger than he. She originally married Earl for his money, and then, when she realized that she was about to lose him to cancer, fell in love with him. Now she feels such a mixture of genuine sorrow and guilt over his imminent death that, as Earl had done, she must flee the house at times—only she always returns. She finds temporary relief in drugs and alcohol. During a consultation with Earl's doctor she learns the terrible fact about the ultimate pain medicine he is prescribing—it will keep at bay the agony of her husband's terrible pain, but, the physician explains, Earl will no longer be the man she has known. The liquid morphine will send him into a vegetative state. This terrible news depresses her so much that she again seeks escape into her own drugs, with near disastrous results.

While Linda is absent, Earl is in the care of Phil Parma, the day nurse from Hospice. He is in good hands. Phil is one of those sensitive men fortunate to have found the profession in which all his personal qualities contribute to make him more than just competent. Phil is the right person in the right place at the right time. The dying Earl needs not just good medical care but also a priest-like person to hear his confession so that he can find absolution for the terrible things he has done. He finds that person in Phil, who listens without judging and offers words of advice and understanding. The blunt, foul-mouthed Earl has established a rapport with Phil; the latter unashamedly at times sheds a tear or two while administering to his charge's physical, emotional, and spiritual needs (though he employs no religious language).

Frank T. J. Mackey is Earl's son, so resentful of Earl that he has taken a different last name. He has become a hot item on the self-improvement lecture circuit, but his philosophy of success is a predatory one based on men holding women in contempt and psychological bondage. We see Frank on TV infomercials and on site at the expensive seminars he holds, attended by men trying to "improve" their prospects with members of the opposite sex. They yell and howl on cue as their guru spews out his jungle, caveman philosophy, setting forth his campaign on how to dominate and humiliate women. Fairly seething with rage, Frank seems like a man headed for self-destruction unless something intervenes to change him and the path of his life. All the above we learn in brief segments before and after the scenes we are focusing on.

The Scenes

Warning: There is some vulgar swearing and "taking of the Lord's name in vain" in this scene—and far more in the other scenes, especially those in which the Tom Cruise character Frank spews out his vicious, misogynistic philosophy at his seminars. Therefore group leaders should use this only with a mature group. For use in a worship service, a paraphrase would be more acceptable than the clip itself. The rain of frogs, borrowed from the Egyptian plagues in Exodus, may also cause some confusion. Because there is so much intercutting of scenes, leaders must see the entire film before using it with a group. They cannot just go to the key scene as in other meditations, because this one depends on the others for full meaning.

Time into film: 0:09:30   Stop at 0:10:35

Phil Parma briskly walks into the living room where Earl lies in the hospital bed that has been set up. Several dogs lie with the sick man on the bed, and the night nurse, also male, is sitting alongside. As the night nurse exits and the dogs hop down from the bed, Phil bends over and greets Earl affectionately. A quick cut-away shows us Earl's lungs, first in animation style, then two X rays of them, one labeled "cancerous." Back to Phil and Earl, and then we see Linda in the bedroom berating their doctor over the telephone and demanding more pain medicine. She walks into the living room, bends over, and tells Earl she loves him and that she is going out for a while. Outside she starts to drive away in their car, but before she does she pounds the steering wheel in frustration and utters the "f" word several times. In the background for most of this scene we hear the song "One is the Loneliest Number."

Fast Forward to 0:19:30   Stop at 0:25:30

Earl talks with Phil, saying, "'Don't want to do this . . . sit here." He says that the dying is not so bad as the getting there and that he feels so useless. "I have a son, you know." Phil picks up on this. At first Earl calls him "Jack." He's not sure where he is, but he is "somewhere around." "He's here in town, but I don't know." He starts to describe his son as "a tough son," but apparently becomes distracted by the thought of their broken relationship, for he asks if Phil has a girlfriend.

When the nurse says, "No," but he's trying, Earl tells him to "do good things with her," that the "b.s." about sharing is true. He then talks about Linda. "She's a good girl. A little nuts," he says. "She loves you," Phil observes. "Maybe," Earl answers, and then shoves any doubt aside with, "Yeah, she's a good one." Phil brings the topic back to the son: "When was the last time you talked with your son?" Earl struggles to recall, "Maybe ten—ten, five—" he almost cries, then says, "that's another thing that goes—" "Your memory?" asks Phil. "The time line," answers Earl. After some tears of frustration and further talk, Earl breaks out coughing. He asks for another pill, and then for a pen. "Want to call Jack, your son?" Phil asks. "His name's Frank Mackey," Earl corrects him, his memory finally kicking in. As the medicine takes hold, Earl says, just before slipping into unconsciousness, "Find him—Ask for—Can't hold on—" At some point, when Frank is mentioned, we hear sounds of an audience applauding and cheering, and then the opening strains of the beginning of "Thus Spake Zarathustra."

The screen fades to black as the grandiose music swells up, and we see a figure on a darkened stage, a white outline around the man's darkened body created by a carefully placed spotlight. As the music rises to its crescendo, the lights slowly come up, revealing more and more of the man standing before a large audience. He slowly raises his arms up and up above him, then dramatically lowers them in sync with the music, pausing once to flex his muscles, as a sign of strength and dominance, before lowering them to his side. At last fully illuminated, the man acknowledges his wildly cheering admirers. The light also reveals the large banner immediately behind him. It proclaims, "Seduce and Destroy." This is Earl's son, Frank Mackey.

Reflection on the Scenes

There are many other scenes involving the other characters, including the one already mentioned in which
Linda, feeling so guilty over her past betrayals of her
husband and her inability to help him, takes an over-
dose of medicine and has to be revived at a hospital.
The stories of several other characters, also lonely and
wanting to connect or find escape in destructive ways,
are skillfully interspersed.

Phil's first attempt to reach Frank by phone fails.
Frank takes so long deciding whether or not to take the
call that Phil has been forced to hang up. Linda has
come home and is furious that he has called the son.
She fears that it would not be good for Earl. However,
Frank does learn that his father is dying and decides to
visit him. In a series of scenes interrupted by cutaways
to the other stories, we witness the son's final minutes
with his father. (Should you want to view this scene, go
to 2:31:16 and stop at 2:34:12.)

Frank rings the doorbell, setting off the dogs' barking, and is admitted by Phil. He tells the nurse to keep
the dogs away, or he will "drop kick them," and to
stand back when he goes in to his father. At first he
says he needs a minute to prepare himself and almost
shrinks against the wall. Apparently braced for what
he considers an ordeal, Frank comes to Earl's bedside
and stares at his father. His rage swelling up, he curses
the old man in a series of invectives: "It hurts, doesn't
it? She was in a lot of pain—I was there, Earl!" "You
don't like illness! She waited for you to call—for you
to come! I'm not going to cry for you." But he does
sob. "You can die! I hope it hurts!" More expletives
and sobbing. Earl is almost totally under the influence
of the liquid morphine Phil has injected to ease his

intense pain, but the nurse asserts that he can hear him. Then, his rage ebbing, Frank kneels beside his father's bed.

Fast Forward to 2:41:06   Stop at 2:42:14

Back at Earl's bedside, Frank's body is wracked by sobs. He is still angry, but a new note has entered his stream of expletives, changing their meaning. It is a note of concern. In between his repeated cursing he pleads, "Don't go away." Over and over. The long buried love and concern of a son for a father has re-emerged. The comatose Earl makes no response. Frank's rage and frustration now look very much like Linda's.

There are more cutaways to other characters. Then something bizarre affects all of them and leads to Earl's regaining his consciousness. Frogs begin to fall out of the sky. Hundreds, thousands, then millions of them. In a series of cutaway shots they interrupt some of the characters and almost lead to tragedy as their little bodies make the streets dangerously slippery and smash through windows.

Fast Forward to 2:51:02   Stop at 2:52:07 (Fades to black)

Frank is still bending over his father. But the noise of the frogs thudding against the roof and windows, which starts the dogs' barking, has jolted Earl awake again. Father and son stare at each other. It is obvious that Earl has all his faculties again, except for his ability to speak clearly. He tries to say something. Frank's eyes widen. He says nothing, but it is apparent that the son's rage and resentment have passed. As he watches, the light fades from Earl's eyes and he slips away peacefully. Frank was late, but the reconciliation he wanted deep down has come to pass.

Magnolia can be viewed as an intense meditation

on our need to connect as human beings, of our need for grace, and of the role of chance and providence in the universe. The story of Earl and Frank is a modern twist on Jesus' story of the Father and Two Sons. But this time *both* father and son are prodigals. Earl ventured first into a "far country" of career and business, not just neglecting his wife and son, but actually walking out of their lives when he could no longer bear to see Lily's pain. Little wonder that Frank turned into the misogynist whom we first see spouting his sexist philosophy of domination to an audience—or that he has harbored such rage against his father all through the years. He too is in "a far country" of anger and blame.

It is Phil who takes the role of the loving father of the parable, his concern for his dying patient leading him to lay aside his professional detachment and become involved in his patient's personal affairs. Phil could not heal Earl's body—he could only ease his pain as death approached—but he could be the means for bringing healing to Earl's psyche, his soul. And not only to Earl, but to the suffering son as well. The incident that awakens Earl so that the wordless reconciliation between him and Frank can take place is the almost apocalyptic rain of frogs.

No explanation is offered for this unlikely event—no assertion that "the Lord" sent them, as the author of the biblical Exodus asserts in his tale of Moses' confrontation before the Egyptian Pharaoh. The rain of frogs just happens, like several other bizarre incidents that scriptwriter Paul Thomas Anderson injects into his script. Christians, of course, see things from a different perspective, from that of the viewpoint of a faith held in common with the authors of Exodus. The latter also records some bizarre events, such as the ten plagues and the parting of the Sea of Reeds, the latter at just the moment when the Israelites needed to escape from the pursuing Egyptians. Exodus does note that a sudden east wind sprang up at the propitious moment, but for the authors this natural "explanation" does not "just happen." They draw a conclusion based on faith in a God who cares what happens to his people, who has chosen them for a special mission—"The LORD drove back the sea by a strong east wind all night, and turned the sea into dry land; and the waters were divided" (Exod. 14:21b). Quite a claim, that God would intervene in such a way. No way to prove it. We have just to accept it, or turn away in disbelief at its bizarreness. The same with *Magnolia*.

For Further Reflection

1. How does death bring things into sharper focus, revealing what is really important in our lives? What does this say about the all-too-frequent tendency to shield from the dying any knowledge of their true condition?

2. In the past people prayed for a "good death" and used manuals written to show the way to a good death. How does our concept of a good death differ? (Note how everyone today is always relieved when assured that their loved one's death was quick and painless, and that they did not suffer.) The manuals for the dying were based on the concept that the dying person needed to prepare for death, and therefore a slow death was preferable.

3. Are there unresolved issues in your relationship with parents and others? What does this film say we

should do about them? (You might compare *Field of Dreams*, about a son's anguished desire to connect with the estranged father who died before they could set to right their differences.) How does Paul's assertion "from now on, therefore, we regard no one from a human point of view" work in Frank, making possible reconciliation with his father? How is Phil's role like that of Christ's? In your own disputes with family or others, how does moving beyond the "human point of view" lead to reconciliation?

4. How does your faith help you to deal with these issues? With death itself? At what points in the film can you discern the hand of God? Note how many tender "moments of grace" there are (even more in the case of the policeman, as sensitive in his own way as Phil).

5. Do you find comfort and assurance in the Psalms? Do you have any favorite ones for getting you through difficult, stressful times? Your church hymnal is another wonderful treasure trove of solace and insight: check out verse 3 of the hymn attributed to Gregory the Great, "Kind Maker of the World." How does verse 3 express what Earl is seeking? Which verse speaks especially to you?

HYMN: "Blest Be the Tie That Binds" or "Kind Maker of the World"

A Prayer

Gracious God, in whom we live and move and have our being, we thank you for those stories in which broken relationships are healed—in the Scriptures and in film. We ask for the healing of any brokenness in our own lives; and for the faith that your healing transcends even the end of this life; that in death and in life, we can entrust ourselves and our loved ones to your loving hands. Strengthen in us the faith of our brother Paul who wrote, "Whether we live, or whether we die, we are the Lord's." In the name of the One whom you raised from the dead, even Jesus Christ, we pray. Amen.

25. *Monster's Ball*
When Loving a Father Is Impossible

Thou shalt not bow down thyself to them, nor serve them: for I the LORD thy God am a jealous God, visiting the iniquity of the fathers upon the children unto the third and fourth generation of them that hate me; And shewing mercy unto thousands of them that love me, and keep my commandments.

Exodus 20:5–6 (KJV)

In those days they shall say no more, The fathers have eaten a sour grape, and the children's teeth are set on edge.

But every one shall die for his own iniquity: every man that eateth the sour grape, his teeth shall be set on edge.

Jeremiah 31:29–30 (KJV)

Now large crowds were traveling with him; and he turned and said to them, "Whoever comes to me and does not hate father and mother, wife and children, brothers and sisters, yes, and even life itself, cannot be my disciple. Whoever does not carry the cross and follow me cannot be my disciple."

Luke 14:25–27

Children, obey your parents in the Lord, for this is right. "Honor your father and mother"—this is the first commandment with a promise: "so that it may be well with you and you may live long on the earth."

And, fathers, do not provoke your children to anger, but bring them up in the discipline and instruction of the Lord.

Ephesians 6:1–4

Introduction

Hank is a head guard in a Southern prison preparing his team for the execution of Lawrence, a black prisoner convicted of murder. Hank's live-at-home son Sonny is also a guard and a member of the execution team, but that is about all father and son have in common. Hank is like his invalid father, Buck, prejudiced against all people of color, but somehow Sonny has escaped from his racist heritage and befriended "coloreds," much to the dismay of his elders. When the two young boys of an African American neighbor come looking for Sonny, Hank grabs his gun and runs them off his property. Sonny is unlike his father in another way, in that he hates his job of preparing a man for death. When he botches a rehearsal of the execution, his father sternly lectures him that there must be "no mistakes." However, on the night of the execution Sonny is so upset that he vomits on the walk to the death chamber and is unable to continue with his duties. Back at their house Hank turns on Sonny contemptuously, heaping scorn and disdain on him. The young man quits his job and sulks at home.

Leticia is a not-too-competent waitress at the diner

where Hank eats many of his meals. She is an unhappy woman, not only because she is estranged from her husband but also because she cannot prevent her over-weight son, Tyrell, from sneaking candy into their home and gorging on it. Hank does not know that Leticia is the estranged wife of Lawrence, nor does she know that he is in charge of the team responsible for executing him. Shortly after Lawrence's death a car strikes down Tyrell on a rain-swept road. Hank comes along right afterward and takes mother and son to the hospital, where the boy dies of his injuries. Even though she is black, Hank feels sympathy for her, probably because he is also inwardly grieving over the death of his own son. (Sonny, weighed down by the contempt of his father and grandfather, had shot him-self in front of Hank after a terrible argument between them. Grandfather Buck's only reaction was to snort that the boy was weak. At the grave in their backyard Hank had told the minister that he wanted no cere-mony, just the sound of dirt hitting the coffin.)

Over the next few days Hank sees Leticia at the diner. Although she rebuffs him at first, their mutual grief and extreme loneliness draw them together. She has no car, so Hank offers her rides, and one night he accepts her invitation to come into her home. In a graphic sex scene that probably makes it impossible to use the entire film in a church setting, the once bigoted white man and the hostile black woman join their bod-ies together to discover in each other a comfort that transcends their racial differences. I say "comfort," because it is out of her own desperate need that Leticia begs him to take her. Hank is the one whose need first changes into love. He seems to find a new lease on life, quitting his job at the prison and going out and setting himself up in business by buying a gas station that had been for sale.

It is Hank's father who almost destroys their mutual happiness. Hank has had the black neighbor repair his spare, old pickup truck so that he can give it to Leticia, who has no car of her own to get to work. (This little scene also reveals how far the transformation in Hank has come, the mechanic and he having once argued heatedly over Hank's running the man's two boys off his property when they had tried to visit Sonny.) Leticia is so grateful for her own means of transportation that she stops and buys Hank a new cowboy hat. When she goes to Hank's house, he is not there, but unfortunately Buck is. Eyeing her coldly, he tells her to give the hat box to him and that he will see that his son gets it. A bit hesitant because of his demeanor, Leticia hands it over to him. He opens the box, takes out the hat, and puts it on his own head, admiring it in a mocking voice. He cuts her to the quick with a racial slur about her sexuality, and says that Hank must be just like him. Repulsed and disgusted, Leticia rushes out just as Hank walks up to the house. She will not tell him what is wrong, nor will she stop screaming and fighting off his attempt to keep her from speeding away.

The Scenes

Warning: This film is rated R for language and an intense sexual scene, so leaders should be very careful if they want to use the film or a video clip in worship or a class. The graphic sex scene is not gratuitous but is part of each of the hurting characters' breakthrough from lonely despair to intimacy. In the following scene for this meditation there is no sexual content, but the language of the father is offensive.

Time into film: 1:29:08   Stop at 1:37:35

As Hank resolutely turns toward the house, Buck is on the porch enjoying watching the havoc he has created. "We're family," Buck says, as his son comes up on the porch. "I'm your father—remember that!" Hank does not answer. He just walks by him. "What's your problem?" the old man calls after him. He will soon learn that it is a problem that his son knows how to deal with.

Right after Hank enters their house, the scene jumps to this one in which we see Hank through an office window. He is talking to a woman. "You will take good care of him?" Hank asks, and we realize that he has been making arrangements to transfer Buck to the senior citizen home. Mistaking that the question arises from a close relationship, the administrator says, "You must love him very much." "No," Hank replies, "but he is my father, so there it is."

The scene switches to Buck's newly assigned room. Hank is in the doorway, and his forlorn-looking father is sitting on his bed. Hank tells him that they will be getting him a television set soon. As they talk, Buck observes, "Finally getting rid of me, huh?" "I guess so," his son replies. "I'm stuck," the old man says in self-pity. "Me too," says Hank. The old man is wracked by a cough. "I don't want to go out like this," he complains. "Me neither," Hank replies. He says goodbye and leaves. Irony of ironies, we see in the background that Buck's roommate is a black man.

Back at the house we see various empty rooms. Hank sits changing into work shoes, and then carries a box upstairs. He goes to the restaurant to inform Leticia that he has sent his father away because of the incident, but she is still too hurt and angry to listen. He persists, and she answers that she supposes he wants his pickup back. Hank says no, that he wants her to keep it. He just wants to talk. She spurns him, so he leaves and gazes at her through the window, the scene ending when his own reflection blots out the sight of her.

A paintbrush applies white paint to a wall. It is Hank using it to redecorate the place. Then he is up on a ladder painting a new sign over the door of his gas station. We can see the large block letters that when he is finished will spell "LETICIA'S." Hank's new friend, the African American father, comes up, and they exchange cordial greetings. He asks, "Who's Leticia?" "My girlfriend," Hank replies.

A deputy mounts the porch of Leticia's rented house, knocks on the door, and announces "Sheriff's Department." When, after knocking several times, he gets no response, he takes out a large tool and starts to rip out the lock. This brings Leticia to the door. She tells the man that she now has the overdue rent, but the deputy tells her that he cannot accept money. She must leave. She pleads, but to no avail. He motions to his helpers to follow him in, and the next thing we see is Leticia sitting dejectedly in the yard with her possessions stacked around her. Hank drives up. Cut to a small U-Haul truck with Hank driving, and Leticia following in the pickup. Arriving home, he takes her inside to what is now her room. She says nothing in response to his, "Relax and make yourself comfortable." She sits down, and he goes into the living room to remove the drop cloths from the furniture. The once drab and dingy house has been transformed into a light and airy place, a welcoming place. She sees that he has a couple of Tyrell's boxes, and he tells her that he is taking them upstairs to his son's room. She accompanies him upstairs. She sees the picture of Sonny. Downstairs again, Hank says that he just wants her to be comfortable. "I don't mind sleeping across the hall, if you want me to," he says. She tells him, "No."

Reflection on the Scenes

The two make love, though this time Hank is more solicitous of her pleasure than his own. The road ahead for the two is rocky, with Leticia that same afternoon discovering Hank's role in her husband's execution. However, Hank is slowly becoming what the apostle Paul would have called "a new man in Christ." Hitherto Hank has drifted through his days like a sleepwalker, but in the face of his father's intractable bigotry, the son's decisive action heads him in a new direction. One wonders how his break with his racist past will set with the community, but that, as they say, is another story. For now it is enough to watch the couple sitting together on the back steps eating ice cream. As Leticia's eyes light on Sonny's headstone, alongside that of his mother's, we can see by her face that her lonely desperation is mostly a thing of the past.

Racism is a terrible affliction passed down, in Hank's family, from father to son. It had totally destroyed Buck's soul, turning him into a bitter, even vicious old man. It isolated him from his friendly African American neighbors, then from his liberal grandson, and eventually even from Hank. The latter had a bad case of racism, but it proves not to be quite so terminal. He breaks out of the "sins of the fathers" cycle, so that he becomes like those described by the prophet Jeremiah—his teeth will not be set on edge by the sour grapes eaten by his father. In his immediately taking his father away he also is like those whom Jesus said must "hate his father" in order to become a disciple.

Hank's putting Leticia's welfare first is, at that moment, the equivalent of following Christ.

Hank and Leticia still have a long way to go in leaving their slough of despair behind, but they seem to have made the first, all-important step. Neither has broken through yet to understand the Source of the love that is transforming them. We can only hope that one day they will realize that it is the transcendent love fully revealed in Christ that has gripped the two of them, a "love that will not let (them) go." Put this film alongside the equally difficult to watch, but richly rewarding, *American History X* as that rare film that suggests that racial bigotry can be, with a difficult struggle, defeated—not eliminated entirely within us, but at least overcome so that its corrosive poison can no longer harm our souls and our relationships.

For Further Reflection

1. Some parents have used the commandment "Honor your father and mother" as an argument for strict obedience. How does the apostle Paul modify this in his letter to the Ephesians? How did Buck "provoke to anger" his son? Have you had similar differences with a parent? What meaning do you see in Hank's statement to the administrator of the home who mistakenly thinks that he loves his father: "No, but he is my father, so there it is"?

2. How has racism affected (or "infected") your family and life? How have you dealt with it? Has your understanding of Christ and your church relationships helped you deal with it? How is the animosity between the races in society an example of the sins of the fathers (and mothers) being visited upon the sons (and daughters)? In our past was the church a help or a hindrance,

a part of the solution or a part of the problem of racism?

3. Interracial couples face unique problems in both the north and south of the United States. What are some of these problems that Leticia and Hank will face? How might they in the long run be a part of the solution?

4. A number of phrases and whole stanzas in Brian Wren's wonderful hymn "When Love is Found" relate to this film. Especially look at and reflect on the third stanza, which begins with "When love is tried as loved ones change. . . ." The hymn concludes with a burst of praise to God for love and life in "age or youth, in husband, wife. . . ." (See no. 146 in his book *Piece Together Praise: A Theological Journey:* Hope Pub., Carol Stream, Ill., 1996.) In what "mysterious way" do you see God working in this film?

HYMN: "When Love is Found" or "God Moves in a Mysterious Way"

A Prayer

O God, who has made "of one blood" all peoples and nations, we come away from such a film as this one with mixed feelings—of being wrung out, yet hopeful. We grieve to see how racism still pollutes our minds, resisting the powers of reason, even though slavery was destroyed in the nineteenth century and segregation was dismantled in the twentieth. It seems as if indeed the sins of our fathers and mothers are still being visited upon our nation. Give us the love of Christ who saw men and women not as "Jews," "Samaritans," or "Gentiles," to be kept apart in their respective places, but as children of God who will one day "sit at table" in the kingdom of God. May your Spirit continually massage our hearts, softening any hardness therein caused by racism, that we might further your mission of breaking down barriers and replacing them with love and acceptance. This we ask in Christ's name. Amen.

26. *O Brother, Where Art Thou?*
"Come On In, the Water's Fine!"

Have mercy on me, O God,
    according to your steadfast love;
according to your abundant mercy
    blot out my transgressions.
Wash me thoroughly from my iniquity,
    and cleanse me from my sin.
. . . .
Create in me a clean heart, O God,
    and put a new and right spirit within me.
Do not cast me away from your presence,
    and do not take your holy spirit from me.
Restore to me the joy of your salvation,
    and sustain in me a willing spirit.

Then I will teach transgressors your ways,
    and sinners will return to you.
Deliver me from bloodshed, O God,
    O God of my salvation,
and my tongue will sing aloud of your deliverance.
                                    Psalm 51:1–2, 10–14

Then Jesus came from Galilee to John at the Jordan, to be baptized by him. John would have prevented him, saying, "I need to be baptized by you, and do you come to me?" But Jesus answered him, "Let it be so now; for it is proper for us in this way to fulfill all righteousness."

Then he consented. And when Jesus had been baptized, just as he came up from the water, suddenly the heavens were opened to him and he saw the Spirit of God descending like a dove and alighting on him. And a voice from heaven said, "This is my Son, the Beloved, with whom I am well pleased."

Matthew 3:13–17

Now the eleven disciples went to Galilee, to the mountain to which Jesus had directed them. When they saw him, they worshiped him; but some doubted. And Jesus came and said to them, "All authority in heaven and on earth has been given to me. Go therefore and make disciples of all nations, baptizing them in the name of the Father and of the Son and of the Holy Spirit."

Matthew 28:16–19

For just as the body is one and has many members, and all the members of the body, though many, are one body, so it is with Christ. For in the one Spirit we were all baptized into one body—Jews or Greeks, slaves or free—and we were all made to drink of one Spirit.

1 Corinthians 12:12–13

Introduction

The Coen brothers are noted for their quirkily humorous films about persons just outside the mainstream of society—such as the inept, ex-con husband of a police officer who tries to enlarge his family by kidnapping a baby in *Raising Arizona*; a gold-fish-like screenwriter trying to navigate the shark-filled waters of Hollywood in *Barton Fink*; or the seemingly dumb, small-town policewoman investigating a kidnapping gone horribly wrong in *Fargo*. There are three outsiders in this skewered send-up of Homer's *The Odyssey*—slow-witted Pete and Delmar, and the schemer who talks them into breaking out of prison, Everett Ulysses McGill. Everett, having received word that his estranged wife is about to marry someone else, desperately wants out of prison so that he can reach her before the wedding. Needing help to do so, he has seduced his two friends into helping him by concocting a tale of buried treasure in his yard, which they must reach before the dam the government is building floods the area. His two friends have but a few months of their sentences to serve, but being not too bright and greedy for wealth, they join in the escape plan. After the three run away, they meet a blind seer who tells them that they will achieve their goal but not as they plan. Shortly after, the following scene plays out.

The Scene

Warning: Mild profanity (by Hollywood standards) earns this film its PG-13 rating. There is in this scene an expletive uttered by George Clooney's character, surprised that his friend Delmar is wading out in the river to be baptized, so if you use this meditation with a group, either warn the group of this expletive or use the paraphrase instead of the clip itself.

Time into film: 0:17:10   Stop at 0:20:10

The trio, after a narrow escape from the pursuing police, are now arguing and scheming in the woods. Slowly the sound of ethereal singing is barely heard. A tenor's voice leads the singing: "Oh, Brothers, let's go down / Come on down. . . ." A congregation of white-robed men and women pass by them in the woods.

Their singing is as of angels. The robed figures, paying no attention to the three strangers, approach a river, and then enter it. The three convicts stand watching them in amazement. Only one woman takes notice of them, calling, "Come with us, brothers! Join us and be saved!" Several members of the singing congregation go forward, and the preacher, without any words, baptizes them. Delmar is overcome and wades into the water. His amazed friends comment on what they perceive as foolishness, but Delmar asserts that his sins are now forgiven, even "that Piggly Wiggly I knocked over in Yazoo." The scene ends with the now-forgiven Delmar's invitation, "Come on in, boys, the water's fine!"

Reflection on the Scene

A recent worship service I attended began with this scene projected onto a large screen. What a moving call to worship it made: "Come on in, the water's fine!" And so the life-giving waters of baptism are for people of faith. Delmar might be ignorant, but he has the right theology—all past sin is forgiven in Jesus Christ, baptism being the sign of this forgiveness. It is a sign that can support us well in the midst of the turmoil of life, as well as quietly reassure us when we are at rest. Martin Luther is said to have almost buckled under the terrible strain of leading the Protestant Reformation in Germany. He was attacked by the Pope in a papal bull that labeled him as "the wild boar in Christ's vineyard." He was declared as heretical and challenged by opponents: "How is it that you are right and the combined wisdom of the church for a thousand years is wrong?" they demanded. He was being hunted at times by those who would have tortured and killed him, had they been able to get their hands on him. At such times

Luther resorted to the assertion "I have been baptized, I have been baptized"—meaning that he had been declared a child of God, and therefore of great worth and value, no matter what his society said to him. Luther's identity was shaped by this fact, not by the opinions and declarations of his enemies. Ever so often we too ought to remind ourselves of our own baptism. Many pastors, as they introduce the sacrament, invite all members of the congregation to think about their own baptism and use the vows of the ceremony as a means of renewing their own. A good invitation, as is Delmar's, "Come on in, boys, the water's fine!"

For Further Reflection

1. What do you know of your own baptism? If you have children or grandchildren, what have you told them about theirs? If you seldom have mentioned it, look for a suitable occasion to do so.

2. In your denominational *Book of Worship*, look up the Baptismal Service. Note how water is described in its many forms in Scripture's story of salvation history. (Note: Your church's office might have the *Book of Worship* on CD-ROM, so that the secretary could easily make a copy.)

3. The next time a baptism is celebrated in your church, use the service as a way of renewing your own baptismal vows.

4. Think of some of the storm-tossed waters you have come through: how has God been present for you at such times? How can reflecting upon your own baptism help in such situations?

HYMN: "Just As I Am Without One Plea" or Avery and Marsh's "I Am Baptized"

A Prayer

Gracious God, we thank you that in Christ your love "has broken every barrier down." In our sophistication, we often forget that our faith began with an invitation—sometimes through our parents, who brought us to you for our baptism, and sometimes issued directly to us when we were "of age." We thank you for the welcoming waters of our birth and our baptism. Help us to overcome our shyness or urbane attitude so that your invitation "Come on in, the water's fine" can be issued to others through us. Like Brother Paul, may we never be "ashamed of the gospel," for it is the power of God for salvation to everyone who has faith. We ask this in the name of Jesus, who welcomes all to come to him. Amen.

27. *On the Waterfront* "Christ on the Docks"

> You shall not spread a false report. You shall not join hands with the wicked to act as a malicious witness. You shall not follow a majority in wrongdoing; when you bear witness in a lawsuit, you shall not side with the majority so as to pervert justice.
>
> Exodus 23:1–2

Why, O LORD, do you stand far off?
　Why do you hide yourself in times of trouble?
In arrogance the wicked persecute the poor—
　　let them be caught in the schemes they have
　　　devised.

For the wicked boast of the desires of their heart,
    those greedy for gain curse and renounce the
        Lord.
In the pride of their countenance the wicked say,
      "God will not seek it out";
    all their thoughts are, "There is no God."
. . . .
They sit in ambush in the villages;
    in hiding places they murder the innocent.
Their eyes stealthily watch for the helpless;
    they lurk in secret like a lion in its covert;
they lurk that they may seize the poor;
    they seize the poor and drag them off in their net.

They stoop, they crouch,
    and the helpless fall by their might.
They think in their heart, "God has forgotten,
    he has hidden his face, he will never see it."

Rise up, O Lord; O God, lift up your hand;
    do not forget the oppressed.
. . . .
O Lord, you will hear the desire of the meek;
    you will strengthen their heart, you will incline
        your ear
to do justice for the orphan and the oppressed,
    so that those from earth may strike terror no
        more.

                              Psalm 10:1–4, 8–12, 17–18

"Then the righteous will answer him, 'Lord,
when was it that we saw you hungry and gave
you food, or thirsty and gave you something to
drink? And when was it that we saw you a
stranger and welcomed you, or naked and gave
you clothing? And when was it that we saw you

sick or in prison and visited you?' And the king
will answer them, 'Truly I tell you, just as you did
it to one of the least of these who are members of
my family, you did it to me.'"

Matthew 25:37–40

Introduction

Elia Kazan's great 1954 film deals with the struggle for
the soul of a young man amidst the corruption of the
New Jersey/New York waterfront. Terry Malloy, a
washed-up prizefighter, works as a lackey for Johnny
Friendly, the ruthless leader of the dockworkers'
union. Malloy knows who murdered Joey Doyle, the
stevedore who had intended to testify against the mob
before a Senate antiracketeering committee. The night
before the hearing, Terry had been ordered to call up
to Joey's apartment and lure him up to the roof. From
the street below Terry watched in horror when union
thugs, waiting for Joey, shoved the would-be informant
over the edge of the roof. Terry is upset at such rough
tactics, but he makes no effort to tell the police or to
leave Johnny Friendly's service.

Later, when Joey's sister Edie challenges Father
Barry, her priest, to leave his church building and come
out and see what is happening on the waterfront, the
priest becomes involved in the struggle of the few stevedores willing to consider standing against their union
bosses. He invites the men to meet in his church basement, away from the eyes and ears of Johnny Friendly's
goons. He pledges to the men that he will stand by them
in their fight if they will speak out. One of the men,
"Kayo" Dugan, rises to the priest's challenge, agreeing
to testify at the Senate investigation if the clergyman will
indeed keep his promise. But Johnny Friendly has

friends in government circles, who promptly send him word of Dugan's impending testimony.

The Scene

Time into film: 0:50:50   Stop at 0:57:15

Terry is working with Dugan in the hold of a ship carrying a load of Irish whiskey. Dugan is laughing at his pilferage of two bottles. Terry begins to speak as if to warn him, but Dugan wants no part of this errand boy of the mob. A moment later the huge cargo net full of cases of whiskey falls onto Dugan, crushing him instantly. A coworker yells to get a doctor, but Pop, Joey's father, also working in the hold, declares that it isn't a doctor that he needs, but a priest.

Jump cut to Father Barry, kneeling over the body of "Kayo" Dugan as he finishes giving the last rites. He puts aside his stole and looks up at the men gathered on several decks of the ship above him and the dead man: Johnny Friendly, who had given the signal to kill Dugan; the goons who had followed orders in this and also in the killing of Joey; and several dozen workers. Edie, apparently hearing of the tragedy along with the priest, also has climbed down onto one of the decks.

Father Barry begins by stating that he has come down to keep a promise made to Kayo to stand with him against the mob. Kayo was one of those people who usually could get up from a setback, he says, but not this time. "They fixed him!" he says. The priest then likens what happened on Calvary to what has just occurred on the waterfront. Joey's death, and now Dugan's, is a crucifixion, as is every action of the mob against a good man. During this sermon the camera cuts away briefly for glimpses of the killers and of the stevedores glaring at them.

Father Barry's next words have a visible effect on Terry, who has come closer to Edie:

"Those who sit around and let such things happen," the priest continues, "and who keep silent, are just as guilty of crucifixion as was the Roman soldier who killed Christ." A thug yells to the priest to go back to his church. Father Barry points to the ship and the body, and declares boldly that *this* is his church, and that if they don't think that Christ is here on the waterfront, then they better guess again. He starts to tell them that Christ is lined up with the workers, but a loud voice interrupts, ordering him to get off the dock. Another crook hits the priest with a piece of rotten fruit. Turning to him, Terry declares that he will flatten him if he does that again. Edie sees this, a look of approval on her face.

Father Barry continues by stating that Christ is with the men every morning when the hiring boss puts them through the humiliating process of picking the favored workers and passing over any who has earned the displeasure of the mob. He sees them worrying about food for their families and giving their souls to the mob so they can gain work. A few other missiles fly through the air, and one of them, an empty beer can, hits the priest, cutting his forehead. Edie's father glares upwards, threatening to fight the next man who throws anything.

The priest fearlessly heaps scorn on the mobsters facing him by asking the workers what Christ must think of the crooks in their expensive suits and diamond rings, who do no work but live on their union dues and kickbacks. Like Christ of old denouncing his enemies as hypocrites, Father Barry calls the mobsters a telling name—bloodsuckers—which strikes fire. The same goon who threw a missile at the priest reaches for another one, only this time Terry stops him with a short, hard punch, knocking him to the floor. Edie watches with approval; Johnny and the other mobsters, with surprised displeasure.

Father Barry tells the men that love "of the lousy buck" is the problem with the waterfront: love of money more than their fellow man, forgetting that every man down here is their brother in Christ. He assures them that Christ is with them wherever they are—during the hiring, at work, and in the union hall, and even here, Christ is kneeling beside Nolan. And he is saying to all of them that as they do it to the least person, they do it to Christ. And what they did to Joey and to Dugan, the crooks have done it to them. Only the workers, the priest asserts, do have the power, with God's help, to knock the mobsters out for good. Turning to the dead body of Dugan, Father Barry asks if it's okay, and then strongly says "amen." He makes the sign of the cross, which most of the men and Edie repeat, even the mobsters doing so because of their childhood conditioning.

The crew boss orders the men back to work. Deeply touched, the men begin to comply. The pallet is hoisted up, Father Barry lighting a cigarette as he stands over the body. Viewed from below, it seems like an ascent from death into heaven, the pallet emerging from the dark ship's hold into the bright light of day.

Reflection on the Scene

In a film crammed with powerful moments, this striking scene stands out. Ironically, as scriptwriter Budd Schulberg reveals in his Afterword to his published script, the film's producer Sam Spiegel tried hard to cut the scene from the script because he feared it would be too static. When Elia Kazan assured Spiegel that he would cut to the listeners and make the scene visually interesting, it was agreed that the sermon would stay in. This was a great decision for us viewers, for the scene is one of the boldest affirmations of incarnate theology to be found in a film.

For the priest Christ is no distant historical figure, but a living companion sharing the hardships and the struggle of those on the docks. This sermon takes seriously Jesus' all-too-familiar words in Matthew 25, in which he identifies with those in dire need. As we help such folk, so we help our Lord as well. As we see in the film, Father Barry's challenging words affect Terry. He has been one of those whom the priest had accused of selling their souls to the mob. He had taken their money, and even though he did not like their strong-arm tactics, had looked the other way. Complicated by his growing love for Edie, Terry's conscience is reactivated, with the priest and Edie pulling on one side and Johnny Friendly and Terry's brother, a business manager for the mob, on the opposite side.

The culture also works against Terry's coming forward and revealing what he knows about the mob's evil activities. As children we are told not to be "tattle-tales." At school we call anyone who tells a teacher something that would get another student in trouble a "snitch." Almost all references to informers are negative: squealer, rat, stool pigeon, stoolie, spy, telltale. Little wonder that in the story Terry holds out so long against the impulse to do what he knows is right. His own brother is a member of the mob, and Johnny Friendly has treated him like a son in need of some guidance. The local union mob has been his only family for many years.

Thus the film is about divided loyalties and the dilemma of whether to tell the truth in the face of community pressure to keep quiet. Father Barry makes it plain in his sermon to the men where he believes our loyalty should lie. It is with the Christ of the docks, the Christ who calls us forth to take a stand against corruption and violence, the Christ who expects us to speak out despite the powers arrayed against us. Few of us will be placed in such stark and dangerous circumstances as Terry Malloy, but we too are called to follow the Christ who is present wherever we go—at our office, factory, school, or farm, in our homes and in our community. Just as Christ through Edie challenged Father Barry to come out of his church building and discover a wider church, and as Father Barry in turn challenged Terry, so Christ addresses us to see and follow him beyond our "God-boxes" on Sunday mornings and into the everyday world of the other six days of the week.

For Further Reflection

1. Do you feel that Christ is present with you at various times of the day? How can you keep this feeling strong? By praying? By taking and reading a small copy of the Scriptures at various times? By talking with someone else who is a believer?

2. You may not have seen such gross acts of injustice as Terry Malloy saw, but what wrongs have you seen others commit? Did you do anything about it? Why or why not? What might you have done? Did it mean going against coworkers or neighbors? How is our silence complicity in an act of wrongdoing? (An example of the latter would be the silence of most Germans in 1933 and 1934, when

the Nazis were just beginning their persecution of the Jews.)

3. Look at the words of Fred Pratt Green's fine hymn "The Church of Christ in Every Age." How does Edie's challenge to the priest and his response embody verses 2 and 3?

4. Have you been as angry as Jesus and Father Barry were against wrongdoers? What did you do about it? Make a list of some of the little wrongs that you see: people put down and insulted; malicious gossip about someone; someone stealing credit for someone else's idea or project; a worthy person passed over for promotion or recognition; cheating; stealing company supplies or property; a company violating environmental or safety regulations. What is the cost (in Jesus' terms, "the cross") of taking action or speaking up? Are you willing to pay it? Can you find allies to lend encouragement and support?

5. *What follows is solely for those who will be watching the scene:* Mr. Schulberg had met the priest upon whom he had based his character. The real-life Father Barry was Father John Corrigan, whose "Sermon on the Docks" attacking real-life union corruption is used almost verbatim in the script. Mr. Schulberg learned of the "waterfront priest" from a news article. It was noted earlier that the sermon almost did not make it into the film because producer Sam Spiegel thought that an audience would not sit through a sermon. Would the film have lost some of its power if we did not hear and see Father Barry's big moment? How did Elia Kazan keep his promise to make it visually interesting?

Hymn: "Our Cities Cry to You, O God" or "The Church of Christ in Every Age"

A Prayer

O God of justice and righteousness, despite your giving us the Commandments; despite your sending the prophets to remind us what you require; despite the great teachings of love given us by your Son; and despite the sealing of his teaching by his blood, shed for us on the cross, we still follow our willful ways of seeking and gaining power and wealth at the expense of our neighbors. Forgive us of any complicity in wrongdoing, or for our reluctance to speak up about it or assist those who could put an end to it. Give us convictions worthy of the heritage of Christ and the prophets—and the courage to live and die by them. Keep us from retreating into our church or pious practices and ignoring the injustices, big and small, around us. This we ask in the name of that disturbing man who condemned unrighteous leaders and drove the moneylenders from the temple, Jesus Christ our Lord. Amen.

28. *Paradise Road*
Heavenly Music by the Waters of Babylon

By the rivers of Babylon—
　　there we sat down and there we wept
　　when we remembered Zion.
. . . .
How could we sing the LORD's song
　　in a foreign land?

　　　　　　　　　　　　　　Psalm 137:1, 4

Where can I go from your spirit?
　　Or where can I flee from your presence?
If I ascend to heaven, you are there;

if I make my bed in Sheol, you are there.
                                    Psalm 139:7–8

When they had sung the hymn, they went out to
the Mount of Olives.
                                    Matthew 26:30

Introduction

The power of music to inspire, to soothe and comfort, and to transport the spirit beyond the limitations of circumstances is universally accepted. In the prison film *Shawshank Redemption* an opera aria transports the prisoners beyond their gray walls to a realm of beauty and freedom. Another opera aria in *Philadelphia* becomes a moment when a homophobic lawyer begins to see the human side of the gay client he has been unable to see as a human being. We see the power of music in perhaps the worst of all circumstances, a hellish Japanese prison camp, in Bruce Beresford's fact-based film *Paradise Road*.

A disparate group of women—from Australia, Britain, the United States, and Asia—are thrown together on the island of Sumatra in a Japanese internment camp throughout World War II. Used to a privileged, class-ridden life in colonial society, many of the women are hard-pressed by the filth and squalor of their camp, the scarcity of food and medicine, and above all, the brutal treatment by their guards. Almost everyone becomes sick with some tropical disease or illness stemming from lack of nutrition, the weaker women dying every day.

Two of the women from very different worlds strike up a friendship one night. Adrienne Pargiter is the wife of a colonial official, whereas Margaret Drummond had been a Presbyterian missionary teaching at a mission school in China and serving as a church organist. In their dormitory Margaret comments on the strain from an Elgar work that Adrienne is humming, even joining in with her. Pleased that Margaret recognizes the tune, Adrienne asks her to take a walk with her in the yard of their compound before lights out. She apologizes to the missionary for the snobbery that had kept them from getting to know each other before. Margaret laughs, and the two joke and exchange stories of their past music studies. The scene closes with Margaret suggesting that they might want to form a group to perform music for the benefit of the camp's morale.

When they share their idea with others, they meet with skepticism—the first objection being that they have no instruments. It will be a vocal orchestra, the two friends say, the women using their own voices as the instruments. When it is pointed out that they have no scores, the two tell them that they will provide them. "Here?" someone else acts skeptically, at a place and time when people are dying—a modern version of the psalmist's piteous cry, "How can we sing the LORD's song in a foreign land?" The two friends declare that this is just when they need music the most. Others warm to the idea, and soon Adrienne is busy going around signing up people. Margaret is busy writing down the scores from memory on the backs of old plantation reports. Adrienne admiringly approves of the scores and is taken aback when Margaret tells her that she will be the conductor, because she had had the most training in London. Again, the skeptics complain, this time that there has never been a woman orchestra conductor. The women gather to rehearse, and their project almost ends then and there when the guards rush in to break up the illegal gathering, beating some of the women and overturning their tables and chairs.

Most of the women assume that the orchestra is finished, but they have not understood the iron resolve of the two friends. Margaret and Adrienne meet and rehearse the orchestra section by section, the smaller groups drawing less attention. They stop whenever a lookout spots an approaching guard. Finally the big night when everything is to come together arrives, again the skeptics convinced that the concert will not get off the ground.

The Scene

Time into film: 1:12:35   Stop at 1:17:35

In the dorm most of the women, orchestra members and audience, dress in their ragged best. In small groups of threes and fours the listeners walk to the thatch-roofed lean-to where the orchestra has already gathered. A guard goes to report this activity to the brutal sergeant who has been the nemesis of Adrienne. The skeptics, almost as if they are glad, predict trouble. At the signal from Adrienne the women emit a chord that sounds as if it came from heaven. The soft chord gives way to the opening strain of the glorious "Largo" from Dvorak's "New World Symphony." We see close-ups of the faces of the choir and of the rapt audience. The guard dispatched to stop the proceedings slows up, removing his rifle from his shoulder and laying it down as he sits on the ground.

The camera cuts back and forth between the face of Adrienne and those of the ensemble. She is pleased with the sound and conveys this with a beatific smile. Her charges beam back, negotiating the intricate parts of the music with seemingly little effort. Back in the dorm even the skeptics are now listening, their cynical pessimism melting away with each new chord. The captain and the colonel come out of their bungalow to listen. Neither moves to issue a follow-up to their earlier order. The music rises and falls. The camera, as well as showing the faces of the audience, guards included, also takes us to the dark cemetery where so many of the women have been laid to their final rest, almost as if to show that they too are included in the concert. The movement rises to a climax, softens and slows down, and at last comes to its quiet conclusion. The audience, guards included, breaks into grateful applause.

Reflection on the Scene

Few of us will find ourselves in as desperate straits as the women of the prison camp. And yet we all go through a dark night of the soul. Our "valley of the shadow of death" might be the loss of a loved one, the betrayal of a colleague at the office, the loss of health or wealth or of work. At such moments the psalmist's doubt about singing "the LORD's song in a foreign land" becomes our cry as well. As one of the women in the film wisely observes, it is just *because of* such times, not in spite of them, that we need the uplifting, healing power of music.

The music that Margaret and Adrienne choose is not from a cantata or oratorio, but it is nonetheless "the LORD's song," in that God is the source of all art. Music that so inspires the spirit and enables its makers and listeners to transcend their present wretched bonds is surely as sacred as any written expressly for the sanctuary. The same Spirit that inspired the writers of Scripture and sacred song also inspired Dvorak and the other composers whose works the women perform. (We are told that the women performed four concerts before disease and death so thinned their ranks that there were not enough who could stand and sing.)

Surely one of the great blessings God has bestowed on his creatures is the ability to create and perform music. Some of the mystics have described the creation to have been made while God and the angels sang and danced. We usually think of the announcement to the shepherds of the nativity of Christ as being in the form of song. Just as most of us would think a worship service without music was a cold and barren affair, so we would think that our daily lives without the presence of music would be dull and drab. It might not always be great music, but even the short and relatively simple popular songs issuing from our radios bring a sense of joy and companionship. Older ones may transport us back to better times, evoking memories of a special moment that bring a smile or a tear to our faces.

You might spend a few moments thinking back over the music you enjoy. And then think of a moment when you especially felt the presence of God. I cannot listen to Handel's "Hallelujah Chorus," or any of Mozart's and Beethoven's symphonies, or Simon and Garfunkel's "Bridge Over Troubled Water" without thinking of the power and the love of the Creator God and wanting to send up a brief prayer of thanksgiving. When we are down in spirit, when, as the psalmist observes, we "make our bed in Sheol," even there we will find God, especially when we hum or listen to some inspiring piece of music. In the film *Trip to Bountiful* the lonely, oppressed Carrie Watts keeps her spirit alive by humming favorite hymns to herself throughout the day. Matthew tells us in his Gospel that even on that sorrowful night in the upper room, Jesus and the disciples ended their supper by singing a hymn before going out to the garden of temptation and betrayal. Whether or not a hymn, theirs and Carrie's are good examples for us to follow.

For Further Reflection

1. How has music been a part of your life? Are there particular songs or pieces that you find yourself turning to again and again?

2. Does the music so permeate your soul that you find it difficult to remain still while listening? Do you like to sing or hum along, keep time with your hands, or tap your feet? What emotions and thoughts does music release in you? Do you feel you are a better person afterward, or that you are in better spirits?

3. Do you set aside time to listen to music, either at the beginning or end of the day? Do you have some favorite recordings that enrich your time of devotion? Do you perhaps have on hand a hymnal to use at such times?

4. If your schedule has been so crowded that you find little time for yourself, look for things that can be cut out so that you can take time to be alone with God and your thoughts. Keep on hand (and buy them if you do not own any) several disks with uplifting music, sacred or so-called secular, and begin or end your devotional period with a musical selection. Note how the rest of your activities might be affected by this brief period, if you stick to the practice.

HYMN: "All Creatures of Our God and King" or "Joyful, Joyful, We Adore Thee"

A Prayer

Gracious God, Creator of this world and of all that is beautiful, we thank you for the gift of music, for its power to transport us to realms that are akin to your kingdom. Help us each day to appreciate it and share it and its blessings with others, whether we be at ease in familiar surroundings, or in a strange and alien land. Through your Spirit-inspired music heal our wounded souls and enrich our moments of joy that we might see all of life as a joyful celebration in thanksgiving to you. We ask that you send a special blessing to all who write and perform music. This we ask in the name of the One whom some call "Lord of the Dance," Jesus Christ, our Lord. Amen.

29. *Remember the Titans*
Inspired by the Past

The people came up out of the Jordan on the tenth day of the first month, and they camped in Gilgal on the east border of Jericho. Those twelve stones, which they had taken out of the Jordan, Joshua set up in Gilgal, saying to the Israelites, "When your children ask their parents in time to come, 'What do these stones mean?' then you shall let your children know, 'Israel crossed over the Jordan here on dry ground.' For the LORD your God dried up the waters of the Jordan for you until you crossed over, as the LORD your God did to the Red Sea, which he dried up for us until we crossed over, so that all the peoples of the earth may know that the hand of the LORD is mighty, and so that you may fear the LORD your God forever."

Joshua 4:19–24

This day shall be a day of remembrance for you. You shall celebrate it as a festival to the LORD; throughout your generations you shall observe it as a perpetual ordinance.

Exodus 12:14

O give thanks to the LORD, call on his name,
make known his deeds among the peoples.
Sing to him, sing praises to him;
tell of all his wonderful works.
Glory in his holy name;
let the hearts of those who seek the LORD
rejoice.
Seek the LORD and his strength;
seek his presence continually.
Remember the wonderful works he has done,
his miracles, and the judgments he has uttered,
O offspring of his servant Abraham,
children of Jacob, his chosen ones.

Psalm 105:1–6

When the hour came, he took his place at the table, and the apostles with him. He said to them, "I have eagerly desired to eat this Passover with you before I suffer; for I tell you, I will not eat it until it is fulfilled in the kingdom of God." Then he took a cup, and after giving thanks he said, "Take this and divide it among yourselves; for I tell you that from now on I will not drink of the fruit of the vine until the kingdom of God comes." Then he took a loaf of bread, and when he had given thanks, he broke it and gave it to them, saying, "This is my body, which is given for you. Do this in remembrance of me." And he did the same with the cup after supper, saying,

"This cup that is poured out for you is the new
covenant in my blood."

Luke 22:14–20

Introduction

Memory and remembering are at the heart of the
Judeo-Christian faith, and they are also central to the
film *Remember the Titans.* The title refers not just to a
winning high school football team, but to the process
of the team members overcoming their racial hostili-
ties, a process that eventually spread throughout the
school and then to the once racially divided community itself. Just as it was important for those who came
after Joshua to remember the meaning of the stones he
erected, for the descendents of Moses to remember the
events of the first Passover, and for the followers of
Jesus to remember the significance of shared bread and
wine—so it is important for the people of the city of
Alexandria, Virginia, to remember the 1971 Titans
football team and their winning battle against racism.

In 1971 Alexandria was a city close to going the way
of Watts, Chicago, Newark, and a host of other cities
as African Americans, no longer willing to suffer the
indignities of white racism in silence, demonstrated for
their civil rights. The school authorities relented to the
demands of blacks by bringing in black football coach
Herman Boone—which meant demoting the popular
white coach Bill Yoast. This arrangement appeared to
many to be a losing situation for blacks, with the feelings of both Coach Yoast and his many admirers running high against what seemed to be an unjust move.
Indeed, Coach Boone soon learns that many on the
white school board expect him to fail so that they can

then replace him with Yoast, while at the same time assuring the African American community that they tried to integrate the team leadership. However, they did not take into account the ingenuity and perseverance of Coach Boone, or the resiliency and openness to change of Coach Yoast.

With the white players vowing to remain loyal to Yoast, and the black players certain that the new coach would favor them, Coach Boone from the very start demonstrates that it is the team that matters to him, not the race of the team members. He is as hard on the black players as the white, showing this by his harsh orders and training regimen. He makes the players pair up interracially for the bus ride to their training camp at Gettysburg College, as well as for their dormitory rooms. Through lectures and endless admonitions, he tries to instill in them a sense of loyalty to the team and the game that transcends their racial differences.

At first both black and white players want none of Coach Boone's philosophy. They quarrel, ignore one another on the field, and thereby flub their plays or react too slowly to commands. White players confront their black counterparts in angry debates. Then in the middle of one night, Coach Boone orders everyone, staff included, out of bed for a marathon run.

The Scene

Time into film: 0:30:10   Stop at 0:34:00

The players grumble at this edict. Even Coach Yoast is puzzled at its seeming unreasonableness. He reminds Boone that this is a high school team, not the Marines. Coach Boone gives no heed to any protests. The group runs through the woods until it seems they can run no further. Covered with perspiration, the coach halts them near an open area. Dawn is breaking, and in the half-light we can see monuments.

Coach Boone asks if anybody knows where they are, and someone replies that it's Gettysburg. Boone reminds them that this is where they fought the Battle of Gettysburg, the site where 50,000 men died "fighting the same fight we're still fighting among ourselves today." He describes briefly the carnage, and then invites them to use their imagination to listen to those killed, wiser now in death than they had been alive: "I killed my brother with malice in my heart. Hatred killed my family! Listen. . . ."

Coach Boone urges the group to learn from the dead. He warns them that if they don't come together, "right now," that they too will be destroyed, "just like they were." He tells them that he doesn't care if they like each other. His goal is that they respect each other so that maybe then they will learn to play the game together like men. We can tell from the ways that the camera reveals the faces of the team that finally Coach Boone's words are beginning to sink in.

Reflection on the Scene

Coach Boone would agree with Santayana that those who do not know history are doomed to repeat its mistakes. It is important that we, as individuals and as a people, develop a keen memory of the past. But for the coach, as with the leaders in the biblical passages above, remembering is far more positive than negative. It helps us not only to avoid the mistakes of the past; it also inspires us to correct those mistakes and to move beyond them. It certainly began to work this way for the Titans. In scene after scene of the film, we see whites and blacks arriving at a new understanding and appreciation of each other. Although the players change slowly and grudgingly, their newfound respect, for some, grows into friendship.

This new attitude and relationship between members of once-hostile races faces a difficult test when the team returns home. Many of their classmates, families, and school supporters cannot understand what has transpired among the team members. Believing that the white athletes are betraying their heritage, many in the student body pressure the white players to return to their old ways. Some do, even dropping off the team. Most, however, want so strongly to play football that they resist, staying with the team and their teammates of the opposite race. Slowly, as the newly motivated, and united, Titans win game after game, the rest of the community is affected, eventually coming around to an attitude of tolerance. Today, when someone from outside the community remarks at the spirit of cooperation and respect among the races there, the 1971 Titans are recalled with admiration and appreciation.

Joshua knew that the events his people were passing through would shape them into a special people, if they remembered. Therefore, he commands them to set up the twelve stones, one for each of the tribes (even as in the original flag of the United States there was one star for each of the states), so that they would always remind them of the momentous acts of God that formed them into a nation. Whenever someone would ask, "What is the meaning of these stones?" they were to be ready to tell the story. Earlier in their history, Moses did not wait for the question to be asked. Following God's command, he established the Passover meal, in which the youngest family member was to ask the meaning of the symbolic food and the family patriarch was to recite, through sacred Scripture and story, how God had freed them from Egyptian bondage. Likewise, Jesus established a meal that would both recall his great sacrifice on the cross for humanity and remind the worshipers of their pledge to follow him in all their ways. Most Christian churches display many symbols to remind people of their faith and its great events and teachings—the cross being central, but also wheat, loaves, cups, and grape vines, reminding us of the Sacrament. Ours is not an abstract faith built on general principles, but one established on important historical events in which we believe that God was leading our spiritual ancestors to freedom—the exodus from Egypt, the crossing of the Jordan, and Jesus' last night with his disciples, to summarize the three Scripture passages.

In your home there are probably possessions prized not for their monetary value but for the memories associated with them. Photographs, a scrapbook, medals and trophies, a book, watch, ring, or dish handed down through the family. An old chair might bring to mind the picture of a grandparent or parent who used to sit in it, maybe telling or reading stories to the young. Or maybe there's a drawer full of souvenirs bringing back the good time of a trip to a foreign country—the very word *souvenir* is derived from the French word "to remember." Memories grow out of events and people that shaped our lives and that, when recalled, sustain us still, strengthening our resolve to carry on and live up to the ideals of our heritage. The worst thing that can happen to us is to let those memories slip away, for then we begin to lose our own identity. No wonder that today Alzheimer's disease is one of the most dreaded afflictions.

Alexandrians will not allow bigots to foul their community life as long as they remember the Titans, nor will Jews and Christians be led astray as long as they recall the great events of salvation by observing the meals celebrating them. The psalmists often recited the great events of the past for inspiration, as we see in Psalm 105, wherein the major events chronicled in the books of Genesis and Exodus are recalled. These ancient events are brought into the present through the power of memory. This is a past that is not enslaving but freeing, a past that offers us hope and strength for facing the problems of our own times.

For Further Reflection

1. What objects do you keep because of the powerful memories associated with them?

2. What person, like Coach Boone, influenced your life, perhaps sending you in a direction you would not have gone had that person not entered your life?

3. What memories are you creating in the minds and souls of the young, whether they are your own children or grandchildren, or others? Have you found that teaching in church groups is a rewarding vocation?

4. In the film, racism is the obstacle that must be overcome; has this been a problem for you? Have any of the heroes of the civil rights struggle helped you overcome this? Or was it someone in your own family or church?

HYMN: "According to Thy Gracious Word" or "For All the Saints"

A Prayer

Gracious and ever-loving God, we thank you for the precious gift of memory, by which we recall people and deeds of long ago and recent times. In Scripture and in our own lives we recall your kindness and love, and so we are grateful. As we remember times in our past, we see that you were there, speaking through the people and events that helped to shape us. Save us from spiritual amnesia, so that we might always know who and whose we are. Grant that we may so live and teach that one day others will remember and be grateful for the times they spent with us. Amen.

30. *Secrets and Lies*
The Pain of Family Secrets

> Then the LORD God said, "It is not good that the man should be alone."
>
> Genesis 2:18a

> Make me to know your ways, O LORD;
>   teach me your paths.
> Lead me in your truth, and teach me,
>   for you are the God of my salvation;
>   for you I wait all day long.
>
> Be mindful of your mercy, O LORD, and of your
>   steadfast love,
>   for they have been from of old.
> Do not remember the sins of my youth or my
>   transgressions;
>   according to your steadfast love remember me,
>   for your goodness' sake, O LORD!
>
> Psalm 25:4–7

Remove far from me falsehood and lying;
    give me neither poverty nor riches;
    feed me with the food that I need.

Proverbs 30:8

". . . and you will know the truth, and the truth
    will make you free."

John 8:32

Introduction

Mike Leigh's quest story begins at the funeral of
Hortense's foster mother. Raised in love and security,
the young woman still feels a sense of rejection, since
her birth mother did not keep her. With the help of
a kindly social worker, Hortense learns the identity
of her birth mother, Cynthia, but hesitates to contact
her. When she finally does call, it is at a bad moment
in the poor woman's life. Cynthia has had a fight
with her daughter Roxanne, and the latter has
angrily stalked out of the house. It seems that the
two cannot exchange two words without quarreling.
Roxanne feels fed up with her mother's constant pry-
ing and with having to live with her because her job
as a street cleaner does not pay enough for her to live
on her own.

Thus when Hortense does call, Cynthia does not
want to talk with her. Even if she had felt better, the
shock of hearing from the daughter she had given up
without even having seen her would have been great.
But the two do talk again, and when they meet,
Cynthia is even more shocked. Because she had
refused to see her child at birth, she was not aware that
Hortense is black. She is convinced that the agency

must have made a mistake, until she examines the papers and sees that she indeed must be the mother. She remembers a long forgotten incident with a black sailor—which could have been a rape—at the same time that she had been involved with someone else. The two women become acquainted at a restaurant, and over the next few days talk on the telephone and arrange to get together again. Hortense is a sensitive, caring person, as is Cynthia, so the two enjoy getting to know each other. Cynthia does not tell Roxanne or her brother (whom she talks with infrequently on the telephone—but only when he calls her). Roxanne notices the positive change in her mother, and it is now her turn to ask Cynthia where she is going when her mother leaves to meet with Hortense. Cynthia coyly turns her question aside.

Cynthia's brother Maurice pays her a visit one day. Since his marriage to the class-conscious Monica, brother and sister have drifted apart, something that hurts them both, especially Cynthia. Roxanne's twenty-first birthday is coming up, and Maurice and Monica want to put on a party for her. Cynthia is not sure that Roxanne will come, but she agrees to try to persuade her. We learn that Monica and Maurice have also drifted apart; their once close, loving relationship has become merely a matter of habit and duty. They share a disturbing secret that they harbor from everyone else. In the meantime Cynthia has grown so close to her newfound daughter that she asks if she will go to the party with her—as her *friend*. Hortense refuses at first, thinking she will be an intrusion, but then relents, allowing herself to be persuaded. For her own part Roxanne agrees to come, if she can bring her boyfriend Paul.

The Scene

Time into film: 1:47:40   Stop at 2:07:22

The day of the party arrives, and Monica has thoroughly put their stylish home in order. She is well aware that Cynthia has never set foot in it before. All the guests but Hortense arrive. The others wonder what Cynthia's friend is like. They are startled when she arrives and turns out to be black. She has brought a present for Roxanne and soon is part of the table conversation. All goes well, although Cynthia busies herself too much with serving the others, almost usurping Monica's role of hostess. Hortense and Cynthia let on that they have come to know each other at the factory. The wine has flowed fairly freely, so when Hortense excuses herself to go to the bathroom, Cynthia, on learning that the others like Hortense, blurts out that she is her daughter.

The atmosphere freezes so solid that a knife could carve it. Roxanne does not comprehend at first, and Maurice and Monica comment that Cynthia should have told them before. Hortense comes back to a table of stunned family members struggling to assimilate the news. When Cynthia informs her that she has revealed her identity, Hortense says, "It wasn't supposed to happen like this." Roxanne becomes so upset and angry that she accuses Hortense of ruining her party, whereupon she storms out of the house. Paul goes with her, and then Maurice follows. He manages to convince her to return, but in the meantime Cynthia and Monica have had a falling out about a past inheritance of money. There is further quarreling when the three return; Cynthia accuses her sister-in-law of being selfish because she doesn't want children. Maurice then reveals his own "secret and lie." He reveals that after a long and painful series of tests and operations, Monica has been found to be incapable of bearing children. "We're all in pain," he declares. "Why can't we share our pain? I've spent my entire life trying to make people happy [we have seen him going to great lengths to get the people who come to his photography studio to smile and look their best], and the three people I love the most in the world hate each other's guts. I'm in the middle AND I CAN'T TAKE IT ANY MORE!!!"

Reflection on the Scene

The family of Mike Leigh's film is dysfunctional, but, unfortunately, not atypical. Many families have "secrets and lies" to which they cling. Masks are worn at family gatherings, hiding feelings of resentment or hostility. Or the family might not even come together any more, or if they do, the television set is allowed to dominate the proceedings. The men gather to watch a ball game, and the women congregate in the kitchen to prepare the meal and talk.

We realize that God did not intend for us to live this way when he created families. God's desire is for us to relate in open, loving ways. But for various and sundry reasons we build barriers and don masks to conceal our "secrets and lies." Into the midst of this world of artifice and falsehood comes the God-sent One who calls himself (at least in John's Gospel), "the way, the truth, and the life." By calling us to a new way of living and relating he promises us that we will know the truth, and the truth will set us free. Maurice knows this intuitively, though he cannot yet recognize the power leading him to make his agonized plea to his family as Christ.

As we see in the last scenes of the film, the catharsis at the family gathering does lead to freedom. In bed

Maurice reiterates his love for Monica and his fear that she no longer loves him. She rolls over to face him, asserting, "You don't know how much I love you." And Hortense is visiting Cynthia and Roxanne. The half sisters realize how much they have in common and make plans to go out together, and Roxanne declares that despite their difference in race, she will introduce her as her sister.

For Further Reflection

1. The people of the film are not church attenders, and yet how could the words from Psalm 25 be a fitting prayer for Cynthia? Have you felt that way at times as you think back over past indiscretions and family rifts? Or, if your life has not been so riven, would Psalm 34 be more appropriate?

2. How have you come to regard your own family? Do you see them as a burden to bear or to escape from? Or as a God-given community of mutual support and respect?

3. What can you do to strengthen or renew family ties? Accept and confess hurts and wrongs? Plan gatherings; initiate a round-robin family newsletter? Use the telephone or e-mail more frequently?

HYMN: "Though I May Speak" or "Blest Be the Tie That Binds"

A Prayer

Creator God, you have placed us in families for nurture and support. We thank you for those times when our families have been a source of strength and mutual care. Forgive us when by a deliberate or thoughtless act or word we have injured family members and driven a wedge between ourselves and others; and help us to forgive family members who have similarly injured us. May our family ties be strengthened by our prayers, our thoughts and words, and above all, our actions. In the name of our elder brother Jesus of Nazareth we pray. Amen.

31. *To Kill a Mockingbird* ## "Stand Up, Your Father's Passin'"

Whoever walks in integrity walks securely,
    but whoever follows perverse ways will be
        found out.
                                              Proverbs 10:9

The integrity of the upright guides them,
    but the crookedness of the treacherous
        destroys them.
                                              Proverbs 11:3

A good name is to be chosen rather than great
        riches,
    and favor is better than silver or gold.
                                              Proverbs 22:1

"Blessed are those who hunger and thirst for righteousness, for they will be filled.

   "Blessed are the merciful, for they will receive mercy.

   "Blessed are the pure in heart, for they will see God.

   "Blessed are the peacemakers, for they will be called children of God.

   "Blessed are those who are persecuted for

righteousness' sake, for theirs is the kingdom of heaven.

"Blessed are you when people revile you and persecute you and utter all kinds of evil against you falsely on my account. Rejoice and be glad, for your reward is great in heaven, for in the same way they persecuted the prophets who were before you.

Matthew 5:6–12

Introduction

In this fine adaptation of Harper Lee's novel set in the rural South during the Great Depression, small-town lawyer Atticus Finch risks his reputation by defending Tom Robinson, a black man accused of raping and beating a white woman. Some of the whites in the community think that Atticus ought to put up just a token defense for a "colored man," but it would be impossible for a man like Atticus to do less than his best. During the court testimony it becomes obvious that Mayella Ewell, the victim, is lying. Her low-class father, Bob, often drunk, is the actual rapist and abuser, but he has forced his weak-willed daughter into blaming Tom Robinson. Tom had passed their cabin on his way to work every day, and had often stopped to chop wood for the neglected, abused young woman. Thus he was a likely person to shift the blame to.

As Tom Robinson testifies, he makes a fatal mistake, one that no African American could afford to make in the South of that time. When pressed by the prosecutor as to why he had done chores for Mayella without accepting any money, Tom said that he felt sorry for her. There is a restrained gasp among the people. Tom breaks off his testimony because he realizes from the buzz and the immediate, hostile reaction of the prosecutor that he has unwittingly crossed a boundary that a "colored" man in the South crossed at great peril.

The Scene

Time into film: 1:38:45   Stop at 1:43:04

It is night, and the jury has been out for two hours. Atticus's son Jem and daughter Scout are in the "Colored" balcony with the Rev. Sykes. The white children had not been able to get into the main section of the courtroom because of the huge crowd, so the black minister had taken them upstairs with him. Atticus Finch, who had in his summation appealed to the sense of justice in the jurors, sits at his desk. The courtroom below is still packed, all waiting for what they believe will be a quick decision. They are right. The jury comes in and takes its place. Then Tom is brought in, and last of all the judge enters. The jury pronounces, "We find the defendant guilty as charged."

The jailer puts the handcuffs back on Tom and escorts him to the door. Atticus walks with him, trying to reassure him by saying that he had expected this. He is about to tell him that they will appeal, but Tom is led through the door. He probably has not heard a thing Atticus has said. Atticus returns to the defense table, gathers up his papers and puts them in his briefcase, and starts to walk up the center aisle. The courtroom is now deserted, except for the black people sitting silently in the balcony. Not a one of them has left. Scout is so intent on watching her father that she neither sees nor hears the people getting to their feet in silent tribute as Atticus, unconscious of the sign of respect being paid him, walks up the aisle. "Miss Jean Louise . . . Miss Jean Louise," the Reverend quietly calls Scout by her formal name. "Miss Jean Louise, stand up, your father's passin'."

Reflections on the Scene

Each time I see that scene in the film, or read it in Miss Lee's book (and her novel is that rare book that offers new rewards to anyone wise enough to return to it from time to time), I feel the tingle of a quiet thrill. No medal or presidential citation could ever mean more than that quiet show of respect from the humblest of the citizens of Maycomb, Alabama. Atticus Finch epitomizes the man of integrity celebrated in the book of Proverbs. He has little of the world's riches—at the beginning of the film we see a poor farmer whom he has helped paying him with a sack of nuts—but as this scene proves, he has the "good name" and "favor" that the author of Proverbs declares are "better than silver or gold."

Atticus is so quiet and unassuming that his children are not aware of what a special man their father is. At the beginning of the film Jem is upset with him because his father refuses to join the Methodist baseball team. Atticus tells him that he is too old. Only after Atticus shoots a rabid dog at the request of Sheriff Tate do the two children learn that their father is "the best shot in the county." They both see his courage on display in front of the courthouse when a would-be lynch mob arrives to drag Tom Robinson out of jail. And now they witness the tribute that the courtroom balcony observers offer him. It is a tribute that all might wish for, but one that is received only by those who earn it by living a life of integrity, of respect for all, even of the lowliest of society—a life of risky love that reaches out to anyone in need, regardless of what others might say or do.

For Further Reflection

1. What have you done to support something or someone that is right but not popular with others? Would you rather be in the right than in the majority?

2. Do people accept your word and respect your opinion? Or have you stretched the truth or arranged facts at times to support your position or yourself more than warranted?

3. On what do you spend your time and money? Yourself and your family only? What causes do you support? Safe and popular ones, or some that might be suspect because they favor the poor over the well-to-do and threaten things as they are? When you give or work for a cause, do you expect recognition and honor? Are you willing to do the little things that seldom are noticed, or do you like to be out front?

4. Do you say and do whatever the group you are with does, and then behave differently, even contrarily, with another group? Do you feel superior when helping someone from a different class? Do you see their claims on you as opportunities to serve, or a burden or intrusion?

HYMN: "O Master, Let Me Walk with Thee" or "Help Us Accept Each Other"

A Prayer

Gracious God, Creator of the wise and the foolish, the rich and the poor, we thank you for those you give us as role models. Teach us to be like them, what the great Reformer Luther called "little Christs," instruments of your grace. Give us your Holy Spirit that we might will those things that build others up, to the end that we too will become persons of integrity and love. Through Jesus Christ our Lord. Amen.

Appendix A

Availability of Films

All the films used in this book are available on VHS or DVD. The list below gives the name of the film/video company that distributes the VHS cassette or DVD disc. They should be available at your local video store or public library. The year following the company is the year in which the film was released to theaters, which might be earlier than its video release. The time is according to the information on the video box or as listed in the indispensable book for film lovers, *Videohound's Golden Movie Retriever 2003.*

> *American Beauty.* Rated R. DreamWorks Home Entertainment, 1999. 118 minutes. Sam Mendes, director.
>
> *Babe.* Rated G. Universal, 1995. 91 minutes. Chris Noonan, director.
>
> *Beyond Rangoon.* Rated R. Columbia TriStar Home Video, 1995. 100 minutes. John Boorman, director.
>
> *Broadway Danny Rose.* Rated PG. MGM Home Entertainment, 1984. 85 minutes. Woody Allen, director.
>
> *Chocolat.* Rated R. Miramax Films, 2000. 121 minutes. Lasse Hallstrom, director.

A Civil Action. Rated PG-13. Paramount/ Touchstone, 1998. 115 minutes. Steven Zaillian, director.

The Color Purple. Rated R. Warner Brothers, 1985. 121 minutes. Steven Spielberg, director.

Come See the Paradise. Rated R. CBS Fox Video, 1990. 135 minutes. Alan Parker, director.

Contact. Rated R. Warner Brothers, 1997. 150 minutes. Robert Zemeckis, director.

Dancing at Lughnasa. Rated PG-13. Columbia TriStar Home Video, 1998. 95 minutes. Pat O'Connor, director.

Dogma. Rated R. Columbia TriStar Home Video, 1998. 125 minutes. Kevin Smith, director.

Entertaining Angels. Rated PG. Warner Brothers, 1996. 110 minutes. Michael Rhodes, director.

Erin Brockovich. Rated R. Universal, 2000. 131 minutes. Steven Soderbergh, director.

Fiddler on the Roof. Rated G. MGM Video, 1971. 184 minutes. Norman Jewison, director.

The Fisher King. Rated R. TriStar, 1991. 138 minutes. Terry Gilliam, director.

Fried Green Tomatoes. Rated R. MCA Universal, 1991. 130 minutes. Jon Avnet, director.

Gandhi. Rated PG. Columbia Pictures, 1982. 188 minutes. Richard Attenborough, director.

Harry Potter and the Sorcerer's Stone. Rated

PG. Warner Brothers, 2001. 152 minutes. Chris Columbus, director.

The Horse Whisperer. Rated PG-13. Disney Studios, 1997. 168 minutes. Robert Redford, director.

In the Bedroom. Rated R. Buena Vista Home Video, 2001. 131 minutes. Todd Field, director.

The Iron Giant. Rated PG. Warner Brothers, 1999. 87 minutes. Brad Bird, director.

It's a Wonderful Life. Not Rated. Republic Pictures, 1946. 125 minutes. Frank Capra, director.

Italian For Beginners. Rated R. Miramax, 2001. 112 minutes. Lone Scherig, director.

Magnolia. Rated R. New Line, 1999. 188 minutes. Paul Thomas Anderson, director.

Monster's Ball. Rated R. Lions Gate, 2001. 111 minutes. Marc Forster, director.

O Brother, Where Art Thou? Rated PG-13. 103 minutes. Joel Coen, director.

On the Waterfront. Not Rated. Columbia Pictures, 1954. 108 minutes. Elia Kazan, director.

Paradise Road. Rated R. 20th Century Fox, 1997. 115 minutes. Bruce Beresford, director.

Remember the Titans. Rated PG. Walt Disney Pictures, 2000. 114 minutes. Boaz Yakin, director.

Secrets and Lies. Rated R. 20th Century Fox, 1995. 142 minutes. Mike Leigh, director.

To Kill a Mockingbird. Not Rated. Universal, 1962. 129 minutes. Robert Mulligan, director.

Appendix B

Visual Parables

Many of the meditations in this book appeared originally in the pages of the monthly journal *Visual Parables*. Edited by the author, this twenty-page magazine has a new publisher and a new look, the format now being 8½" x 11". The author reviews current movies relevant to the church, as well as some cable films and those small films that bypass theaters and go directly to video. A United Methodist minister reviews film books and DVDs, and almost every issue includes a film discussion guide. Preachers appreciate the column "Lectionary Links," which connects one or more film scenes to a Scripture passage in the Common Lectionary. "Praying the Movies" appears about eight or nine times a year, along with reviews of short videos useful for church school classes and group studies. For a sample copy send three postage stamps and an address label to *Visual Parables*, P.O. Box 370, Walton, KY 41094.

Appendix C

Building a Video Library

When I first began using films as part of my teaching ministry, they were available only on 16-mm film. They were expensive to rent ($50 to $300) and impossible to own, unless you were wealthy. If anything pushed me into violating the Tenth Commandment, it was reading about some entrepreneur who owned a collection of films and a screening room. Then came VHS, and owning a film was no longer an impossible dream. Today many individuals boast of hundreds of films in their collection. I own two or three hundred myself, carefully selected (lack of space makes one very discriminatory), mostly bought "used" at video stores, garage sales, or flea markets.

Some churches are also adding videos to their libraries, their leaders realizing that often a person or family might be as likely to watch a video as read a book. When I led a workshop in a church in the eastern part of the country, I was pleased to see that the librarian copied the review of the film from *Visual Parables* and inserted it into the video box. Thus potential viewers could read the review not only for the plot but also for some tips as to how the film might connect with the faith. To decide what films to buy for such a collection, start with the list contained in this book, then the list from the first edition of *Praying the Movies*, and then add those on the annotated list below.

Amadeus—Not good history, but a wonderful parable about grace in the life of Mozart from the standpoint of the disappointed composer Salieri and his warfare with God.

Boyz 'N the Hood—A good glimpse into the life of an urban black youth faced with the choice between violence and peace.

Citizen Kane—A great movie about the effects of the lack of love and a visual parable of sin as separation.

A Bronx Tale—Good parable on a father as a role model and the costs of racism and reliance on fear to gain respect.

Chariots of Fire—Based on Scots Olympic runner Eric Liddell, the film shows the integrity and courage required to hold onto one's faith-based values.

Crimes and Misdemeanors—This Woody Allen masterpiece deals with a man's choice between good and evil and the result of choosing the latter in what seems to be an indifferent universe.

Eleni—Set in the mountains during the Greek civil war, this film is the true story of a mother's sacrifice for her children and the consequences of her heritage of love.

The Long Walk Home—A warm story set during the Montgomery Bus Boycott about a black mother having to walk miles to her job as a maid and the effect she has on the white woman who employs her.

Philadelphia—Ironic story of a homophobic African American lawyer who at first rejects the case of an AIDS victim, and then reconsiders and moves beyond his old ways when he gets to know his client.

Saint of Fort Washington—A powerful drama of two homeless men, one of whom might indeed be a "saint."

Unforgiven—Set in the old West, this film is a stark parable of the effects of not forgiving and of the repercussions of violence.

The Year of Living Dangerously—Set in Indonesia during the last months of the dictatorial Sukarno regime, this features an unusual Christ figure who opens the eyes of an Australian journalist to the plight of the poor.

This is a list of what might be called "must have" films. There are many, many others that could be included—and remember, the sixty films featured in my two books are also to be included. I have compiled, as a handout at my film workshops, a list of over 450 films arranged according to several theological categories. Readers interested in this list may obtain a copy by sending a quarter and a SASE to *Visual Parables*, P.O. Box 370, Walton, KY 41094.